I0831081

SPIRITS
of
'76

SPIRITS of '76

Celebrating 250 Years with Cocktails from Every State

KIM LAIDLAW

weldonowen

CONTENTS

Celebrating AMERICA'S SEMIQUINCENTENNIAL

In celebration of America's semiquincentennial—the 250th anniversary of the signing of the Declaration of Independence—we invite you to raise a glass to the spirit, history, and diversity that define the United States.

This special cocktail collection features 102 inspired recipes from all 50 states and Washington, DC, each one capturing the unique character of its origin. As we approach this historic milestone, let us reflect on where we've been, honor the people who shaped our journey, and toast to the future we are building together.

From iconic classics to inventive modern creations, these drinks are as varied and vibrant as America itself. Sip on a timeless Manhattan (page 140) from New York or a bracing Mint Julep (page 80) from Kentucky. Explore regional flair with the Blue Hawaii (page 56) from the Aloha State or the zesty Orange Crush (page 44) of Delaware. Discover new favorites like the botanical-forward Oregon Rose Fizz (page 163), the smoky Smoked Sweet Home Sour (page 19) from Alabama, or the wild and wonderful Midnight Mycelium (page 167) from Pennsylvania.

Whether you're a seasoned mixologist or simply raising a glass with friends, this book offers something for every taste—bold bourbons, crisp citrus, herbal gin, fruit-forward fizzes, and even unexpected ingredients like spruce tips, American persimmons, or wild huckleberries. Each recipe tells a story, celebrating the land, people, and traditions that shaped it—a tribute to the rich cultural tapestry that defines our nation.

Join us on this spirited journey across the country—one cocktail at a time—and toast to 250 years of freedom, flavor, and the American spirit.

BAR TOOLS

Whether you're mixing up a classic cocktail or experimenting with new creations, the right tools make all the difference. From precision measuring to perfect garnishes, these bar essentials will help you craft drinks with confidence and style.

MEASURING CUPS AND SPOONS

Precision is key in mixology, and small glass cups designed for measuring liquids will help you measure ingredients down to the ounce. Make sure to use a set that measures in ounces, as the recipes in this book use measures ranging from ⅛ ounce to 4 or more ounces.

BAR SPOON

Also called a cocktail spoon, this long-handled stirrer is used for gently mixing drinks in a shaker or glass. Its slim profile also makes it handy for layering ingredients or muddling small garnishes.

MUDDLER

Shaped like a mini baseball bat, this bar tool is designed for gently mashing fruits, herbs, or sugar cubes to release their flavors. Opt for a flat-headed, solid-wood muddler that's long enough to reach the bottom of your cocktail shaker or glass.

CHANNEL KNIFE

This small, specialized tool features a sharp, V-shaped blade that carves long, curly strips of citrus peel—perfect for eye-catching garnishes.

JUICERS

A must-have for crafting cocktails with fresh citrus, juicers come in a variety of forms. Handheld squeezers work best for lemons and limes, while larger citrus fruits, such as oranges and grapefruits, benefit from a sturdy reamer.

COCKTAIL SHAKER

A staple of any bar setup, the cocktail shaker is your go-to for blending and chilling ingredients quickly. Whether you're making a frothy sour or a classic daiquiri, this tool delivers consistent results and a well-balanced pour.

STRAINER

Designed to keep ice and solids in the shaker while you pour, a good strainer ensures a smooth, clean cocktail in the glass.

HAWTHORNE STRAINER

Recognized by the coil spring around its edge, this strainer fits snugly over most cocktail shakers and mixing glasses. It's a versatile choice for straining both shaken and stirred drinks with ease.

COCKTAIL PICKS

Used for spearing olives, cherries, or citrus twists, cocktail picks add both function and flair to your garnishes. They're a simple way to elevate your presentation.

ICE BUCKET AND TONGS

Keep your ice close and your service smooth. An insulated bucket with tongs ensures you always have cold cubes ready and never need to touch them by hand.

GLASSWARE

The right glass enhances more than presentation—it plays a key role in how a cocktail looks, smells, and tastes. Each glass is designed with a purpose: to keep drinks cold, concentrate aromas, showcase bubbles, or highlight clarity. From a rocks glass for your old-fashioned or Negroni to a coupe for your daquiri or a highball for a soda-topped smash, the proper glass elevates both the experience and the drink itself.

COLLINS GLASS

Similar to a highball but slightly taller and narrower, the collins glass—named after the Tom Collins cocktail—is great for drinks that benefit from a long, cool presentation.

COPPER MUG

Best known as the signature mug for mules, this metallic vessel isn't just stylish—it's great for keeping icy, fizzy drinks cold and refreshing.

COUPE GLASS

Featuring a wide, shallow bowl, the coupe is best suited for cocktails that are shaken or stirred and served without ice. It brings vintage charm to classic concoctions.

HIGHBALL GLASS

Tall and slim, this glass is perfect for fizzy cocktails. Its shape helps preserve carbonation, making it a favorite for refreshing drinks served over ice.

MARTINI GLASS

With a sleek, V-shaped design, this elegant stemmed glass is the go-to choice for cocktails served "up"—that is, chilled and strained without ice, like a classic martini.

NICK AND NORA GLASS

This petite stemmed glass offers vintage sophistication with a compact bowl that's perfect for smaller, spirit-forward cocktails. It's named after the stylish sleuths in the *Thin Man* films and ideal for elegantly served drinks without ice.

PINT GLASS

This versatile, straight-sided glass is most often used for beer but works just as well for casual mixed drinks or even soft drinks.

ROCKS GLASS

Also called an old-fashioned glass, this short, sturdy tumbler is ideal for spirits served over ice. It's the classic vessel for whiskey and slow-sipping cocktails.

MIXERS

Just as a well-crafted dish relies on fresh, quality ingredients, a great cocktail is built on the foundation of exceptional mixers. Each element brings its own layer of complexity and personality to a drink, from the brightness of fresh citrus to the herbal notes in a carefully selected vermouth. While classic cocktail recipes will always be go-tos, changing up even a single ingredient can breathe new life into a familiar drink, transforming it into something entirely fresh and exciting.

The cocktails in this book celebrate the diverse flavors and influences of specific regions across America, highlighting iconic ingredients and mixers rooted in each state. From the fiery heat of Southwest chiles and the earthy sage and pine of the Central Plains to the sweet, succulent berries of the Pacific Northwest and the juicy peaches of the South, the regional influences on cocktail-making are as rich and varied as the landscapes themselves.

AROMATIC BITTERS

These concentrated flavor enhancers are made by infusing aromatic plants, spices, or citrus peels in alcohol. Though traditionally bitter, they contribute essential complexity and depth to a cocktail. Angostura and orange bitters are classic options, but you can experiment with regional varieties—peach bitters for a modern sweet-tea based cocktail from Georgia, or black walnut bitters for an apple-based old-fashioned from Arkansas—for a truly local touch.

LIQUEURS

Liqueurs, crafted from distilled spirits combined with fruit, herbs, or spices, are a cornerstone of many cocktails. With less alcohol and more sugar than traditional spirits, they bring both sweetness and flavor to a drink. Classic orange liqueurs like Cointreau and Grand Marnier are staples, but regional liqueurs—such as blackberry from the Pacific Northwest or cherry from Michigan—add a distinctive local character to the cocktails in this book.

VERMOUTH

A fortified wine flavored with botanicals, vermouth is a key ingredient in many iconic cocktails, from martinis to Negronis. Sweet vermouth, often associated with Italy, and dry vermouth, typically from France, each brings its own unique profile. But don't overlook vermouths made closer to home—American vermouths from states like California are gaining attention for their balanced flavors and regional botanicals, offering a new take on this classic ingredient.

SIMPLE SYRUPS

Simple syrup is the workhorse of the cocktail world, offering sweetness and balance in a wide variety of drinks. While the basic version is made from sugar and water, infusing syrups with herbs, spices, or fruits can add layers of flavor. From basil-mint syrup and a wide array of berry syrups to localized versions like toasted Carolina Gold rice syrup from North Carolina or huckleberry syrup from Wyoming, these syrups bring regional flavors into the mix, making each drink feel deeply connected to its origins. Adjust the amount of syrup in your cocktail depending on how sweet (or tart) you like your drink.

FRESH JUICES AND FRUIT PUREES

Fresh juice is the lifeblood of many cocktails, bringing brightness, acidity, and fragrance to every sip. The best cocktails use freshly squeezed citrus—lemons, limes, and oranges—whenever possible. But the book also highlights the use of other regional juices, such as tart cranberry juice from Massachusetts, pineapple juice from Hawaii, or pomegranate juice from California. Fresh fruit purees, such as peach from Georgia, pawpaw from West Virginia, or prickly pear from Arizona, can also lend vibrant sweetness and texture to a drink, elevating it with local, seasonal ingredients.

SHRUBS

Shrubs—drinking vinegars made from fruit, sugar, and vinegar—are one of the most unique and historically rooted mixers in the cocktail world. Offering a tangy, sweet contrast, shrubs are making a resurgence in bars across the country. These mixers are often crafted with locally grown fruits, such as wild plums from South Dakota or apples from Missouri, creating a delicious regional twist on both classic and modern cocktails.

OTHER DRINKS

Ginger beer, sodas, lemonade, and even coffee or tea can all play a crucial role in building unique cocktails. Some of the drinks in this book incorporate locally produced sodas, such as Moxie from Maine or Vernors Ginger Soda from Michigan, which add local flair and effervescence. Additionally, beverages like lemonade, cold brew coffee, or sweet iced tea are used to introduce flavor and a refreshing kick, perfect for summer or anytime you need a bold, thirst-quenching cocktail.

MAKES 1 DRINK

Classic ALABAMA SLAMMER

The Alabama slammer, a bold, fruity Southern classic, is said to have originated at the University of Alabama in the 1970s. With whiskey, sloe gin, and amaretto, this cocktail embodies the state's love for rich flavors and spirited traditions.

- 2 ounces fresh orange juice
- 1 ounce Southern Comfort, whiskey, or bourbon
- 1 ounce sloe gin
- ¾ ounce amaretto or other almond liqueur
- 1 maraschino cherry, for garnish
- 1 orange slice, for garnish

Fill a cocktail shaker with ice, then add the orange juice, whiskey, sloe gin, and amaretto. Cover and shake vigorously until chilled. Fill a collins glass half full of ice. Strain into the glass and serve, garnished with the cherry and orange slice.

MAKES 1 DRINK

Modern
SMOKED SWEET HOME SOUR

A modern nod to some of Alabama's favorite flavors, this cocktail combines bourbon, local honey, and toasted pecan bitters. The smoky finish captured from the wood chip elevates this smooth, Southern-inspired cocktail with layered complexity.

---

1 small wood chip, such as apple, cherry, or pecan, for smoking

2 ounces bourbon

¾ ounce fresh lemon juice

½ ounce Honey Simple Syrup (page 224), preferably made with Alabama honey

2 dashes toasted pecan or black walnut bitters, plus more for garnish

½ ounce egg white

Place the wood chip on a small, flame-proof surface (such as a small cast-iron pan). Light the wood chip. When the chip begins to smoke, invert a chilled rocks glass over the burning wood chip to trap the smoke.

Meanwhile, make the cocktail. Add the bourbon, lemon juice, simple syrup, bitters, and egg white to a cocktail shaker and shake vigorously for 30 seconds. Fill the shaker with ice, cover, and continue to shake until well chilled and frothy.

Remove the rocks glass from over the wood chip and turn it right side up. Strain the cocktail into a glass. Garnish the froth with a few drops of bitters.

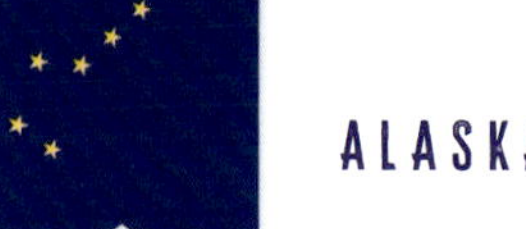

ALASKA

MAKES 1 DRINK

Classic
DUCK FART

The Duck Fart is Alaska's signature shot, said to have originated at a bar in Anchorage. This layered libation—bold whiskey, smooth Baileys, and rich coffee liqueur—mirrors the state's rugged yet comforting spirit, perfect for toasting under the northern lights.

- ½ ounce coffee liqueur, preferably Kahlúa
- ½ ounce Baileys Original Irish Cream
- ½ ounce whiskey

Pour the coffee liqueur into a 2-ounce shot glass. Hold a bar spoon diagonally over the coffee liqueur so the tip of the spoon touches the side of the glass and the back side of the spoon faces up. Very slowly pour the Irish cream over the back of the spoon to create a distinct layer. Repeat to pour the whiskey over the spoon into the glass, creating a third distinct layer. Serve at once.

MAKES 1 DRINK

Modern SPRUCE COLLINS

The Spruce Collins captures Alaska's wild essence, blending juniper-rich gin with tart lemon and fragrant spruce tips. You can also use fir tips, but be careful not to use leaves from the yew plant, as they are toxic. Inspired by the state's vast forests and crisp air, this refreshing twist on a classic Tom Collins is a toast to the Last Frontier's untamed beauty.

---

2 ounces juniper-forward gin

1 ounce fresh lemon juice

¾ ounce Spruce Tip Simple Syrup (page 223)

4 ounces club soda or sparkling water

1 thin lemon slice, for garnish

1 spruce sprig, for garnish

Fill a cocktail shaker with ice, then add the gin, lemon juice, and simple syrup. Cover and shake vigorously until chilled. Strain into an ice-filled collins glass. Top with the club soda and stir. Garnish with the lemon slice and spruce sprig.

MAKES 1 DRINK

Classic TEQUILA SUNRISE

The tequila sunrise, with its vibrant layers, echoes Arizona's breathtaking desert sunrises. Though popularized in California, this iconic cocktail was first crafted at the Arizona Biltmore hotel in the 1930s, making it a true Southwestern classic with a history as rich as its hues.

- 2 ounces blanco tequila
- 3 ounces fresh orange juice
- 2 ounces pineapple juice
- ½ ounce grenadine
- 1 slice orange, for garnish
- 1 or 2 chunks of pineapple, for garnish

Fill a chilled highball glass with ice, then add the tequila, orange juice, and pineapple juice. Stir gently with a bar spoon. Slowly pour the grenadine into the cocktail; it will sink to the bottom to create a layered effect. Spear the orange slice and pineapple chunk(s) with a cocktail pick and garnish.

MAKES 1 DRINK

Modern PRICKLY HEAT MARGARITA

This bold Arizona-inspired margarita blends smoky mezcal with sweet prickly pear and a spicy chile-salt rim for a modern variation. Reflecting the desert's vibrant colors and fiery sunsets, it offers a perfect balance of heat and sweetness, capturing the essence of the Grand Canyon State. Look for prickly pear syrup at a well-stocked beverage store or online.

- ½ teaspoon kosher salt, for rimming the glass
- ¼ teaspoon chile powder or chile-lime seasoning, for rimming the glass
- 2 lime wedges
- 2 ounces mezcal or tequila blanco
- 1 ounce prickly pear–infused syrup
- 1 ounce fresh lime juice
- 1 ounce fresh orange juice

Pour the salt and chile powder onto a small plate and stir to combine. Gently rub 1 of the lime wedges around the rim of a rocks glass. Holding the base of the glass, dip the rim into the chile salt. Fill the glass halfway with ice.

Fill a cocktail shaker with ice. Add the mezcal, prickly pear syrup, lime juice, and orange juice. Cover and shake vigorously until chilled. Strain into the glass. Garnish with the remaining lime wedge and serve.

ARKANSAS

MAKES 1 DRINK

Classic

ARKANSAS LEMON GINGER SHANDY

A refreshing nod to Arkansas's deep love of beer, this citrusy shandy is perfect for tailgating and warm Southern nights. Blending light beer, lemonade, and ginger ale, it's a crisp, easygoing drink made for cheering on the Razorbacks in style.

8 ounces cold light beer or ale
3 ounces cold ginger ale
3 ounces cold lemonade
1 lemon slice, for garnish

Add the beer, ginger ale, and lemonade to a pint glass. Stir gently, then garnish with the lemon slice. Serve.

MAKES 1 DRINK

Modern BLACK APPLE OLD-FASHIONED

A bold twist on the old-fashioned, this cocktail celebrates Arkansas's heritage with the deep, tart flavors of Arkansas Black apples. Muddled with black walnut bitters and sweet apple syrup, it's a drink that packs the perfect Southern punch.

- 2 apple slices, cored, preferably Arkansas Black apple
- ¾ ounce Cinnamon-Apple Simple Syrup (page 227)
- 3 dashes black walnut bitters
- 2½ ounces bourbon

In an old-fashioned glass, muddle 1 apple slice with the apple syrup and bitters. Fill the glass with ice cubes. Add the bourbon and stir. Garnish with the remaining apple slice and serve.

MAKES 1 DRINK

Classic MAI TAI

Created at Trader Vic's in California, the mai tai is one of the state's most iconic cocktails and a tiki staple, deeply linked to Hawaiian cocktail culture. With its vibrant blend of rum, citrus, and almond liqueur, this tropical classic showcases the bold, balanced flavors that define the genre.

- 1½ ounces white rum
- 1 ounce dark rum
- 1 ounce fresh lime juice
- ¾ ounce orange curaçao or other orange liqueur
- ¾ ounce almond liqueur, preferably L'Orgeat
- 1 lime wheel, for garnish
- 1 maraschino cherry, for garnish
- 1 mint sprig, for garnish

Fill a cocktail shaker with ice, then add both rums, the lime juice, the orange curaçao, and the almond liqueur. Cover and shake vigorously until chilled. Fill a rocks glass with crushed ice. Strain into the glass. Garnish with the lime wheel, cherry, and mint.

MAKES 1 DRINK

Modern PISCO SOLSTICE

The Pisco Solstice reinvents San Francisco's legendary Pisco Punch with a bold, modern edge. Bright yuzu and a tangy pineapple-pomegranate shrub add layered complexity, bringing a contemporary twist to this Gold Rush–era classic once beloved by nineteenth-century fortune seekers.

- 2 ounces pisco
- 2 ounces Pineapple-Pomegranate Shrub (page 229) or pineapple juice
- 1½ ounces yuzu or lemon juice
- 2 dashes orange bitters
- 3 ounces club soda
- Edible flowers, for garnish

Fill a cocktail shaker with ice, then add the pisco, shrub, yuzu juice, and orange bitters. Cover and shake vigorously until chilled. Fill a highball glass with ice. Strain into the glass. Top with the club soda. Garnish with the edible flowers.

MAKES 1 DRINK

Classic
COLORADO BULLDOG

A smooth variation of the White Russian, this popular creamy, cola-spiked cocktail is said to have ties to Colorado's lively bar scene, although its origins are unclear. The added fizz gives it a refreshing edge, making it a favorite for those who enjoy a rich yet drinkable classic.

- 1 ounce coffee liqueur, preferably Kahlúa
- 1 ounce vodka
- 1 ounce half-and-half
- 2 ounces cola, preferably Coca-Cola

Fill a cocktail shaker with ice, then add the coffee liqueur, vodka, and cream. Cover and shake vigorously until chilled. Fill a rocks glass with ice. Strain into the glass. Top with the cola and serve.

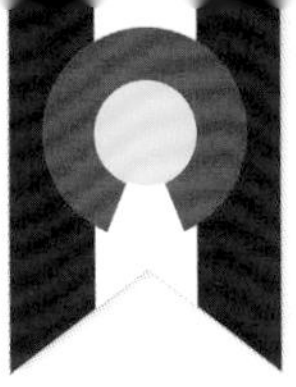

MAKES 1 DRINK

Modern

HIGH ALPINE HAZE

Inspired by Colorado's rugged peaks and wild terrain, this vibrant cocktail balances botanical gin with tart huckleberries and aromatic sage—a defining feature of the state's landscape, especially in its vast sagebrush plains and foothills. A splash of citrus and sparkling wine adds crisp elevation, echoing the bright, refreshing air of the high country.

---

2 tablespoons fresh huckleberries or blueberries

½ ounce Honey-Sage Simple Syrup (page 224)

1½ ounces botanical gin

1 ounce fresh grapefruit juice

2 ounces sparkling white or rosé wine

Fresh sage leaves, for garnish

In a cocktail shaker, muddle the huckleberries with the syrup. Fill the shaker with ice and add the gin and grapefruit juice. Cover and shake vigorously until chilled. Strain into a wine glass. Top with the sparkling wine and gently stir with a bar spoon. Smack a fresh sage leaf, then float it on top.

MAKES 1 DRINK

Classic MOSCOW MULE

Though invented in a Los Angeles bar, this crisp mix of vodka, lime, and ginger beer owes its fame to Connecticut. John Martin, president of Hartford's Heublein company, had recently acquired Smirnoff but struggled to sell vodka. Partnering with Cock'n Bull Ginger Beer owner Jack Morgan and Russian immigrant Sophie Berezinski—who had a surplus of copper mugs—he helped create the Moscow mule. Martin then brought the drink back to Connecticut, using Heublein's marketing power—photographing bartenders nationwide serving it in copper mugs—to popularize vodka in America. Thanks to Connecticut's influence, this once-obscure spirit became a staple, and the Moscow mule remains a refreshing classic.

---

2 ounces vodka
3 to 4 ounces ginger beer
1 ounce lime juice
Crushed ice
1 fresh mint leaf, for garnish

Pour the vodka, ginger beer, and lime juice into a copper mug or a highball glass. Add ice and stir well. Garnish with a mint leaf and serve.

MAKES 1 DRINK

Modern WHITE BIRCH FIZZ

Named for Connecticut's striking white birch trees, this cocktail reflects the state's natural beauty and colonial heritage. Botanical gin and apricot brandy are a nod to New England's orchards, while silky egg white and warming nutmeg evoke the cozy charm of historic taverns and autumn forests.

- 2 ounces botanical gin
- ¾ ounce apricot brandy
- ¾ ounce fresh lemon juice
- ½ ounce Honey Simple Syrup (page 224)
- ½ ounce egg white
- Freshly grated nutmeg, for garnish

Add the gin, brandy, lemon juice, syrup, and egg white to a cocktail shaker. Cover and shake vigorously for 30 seconds. Fill the shaker with ice, cover, and continue to shake until well chilled and frothy. Strain into a chilled coupe glass and garnish with a grating of nutmeg.

MAKES 1 DRINK

Classic ORANGE CRUSH

Bright, citrusy, and synonymous with summer, the orange crush is a coastal icon with deep ties to Delaware's beach culture. First mixed in Ocean City, Maryland, it was perfected in Dewey Beach, becoming a beloved local tradition. In 2024, Delaware cemented its legacy by officially declaring it the state cocktail when the governor signed House Bill No. 444 into law.

Crushed ice

2 ounces orange vodka

1 ounce orange liqueur, preferably triple sec

Freshly squeezed juice of 1 navel orange (or ¼ cup fresh orange juice)

3 ounces lemon-lime soda, preferably Sierra Mist or Sprite

1 orange slice, for garnish

Fill a pint glass two-thirds full of crushed ice. Add the vodka and orange liqueur, then add the orange juice. Top with the lemon-lime soda. Garnish with a straw and an orange wedge.

DECEMBER 7, 1787

MAKES 1 DRINK

Modern
WATERMELON-LIME SHANDY

Refreshing and bright, this updated twist on a classic shandy celebrates Delaware's craft beer heritage and coastal flavors. Featuring Dogfish Head ale, fresh watermelon juice, and lime, this crisp, summery drink embodies the state's innovative brewing spirit and love for beachside sipping.

---

10 ounces cold ale, preferably Dogfish Head

4 ounces cold watermelon juice

1 ounce lime juice

1 cucumber ribbon

3 small watermelon balls or 1 small watermelon wedge, for garnish

---

Add the beer, watermelon juice, and lime juice to a pint glass. Stir gently. Weave the cucumber ribbon around the watermelon balls. Spear on a cocktail pick and garnish. Alternatively, garnish with a watermelon wedge. Serve.

MAKES 1 DRINK

Classic
FROZEN KEY LIME DAIQUIRI

A tart, tropical homage to Florida's famed key limes and Cuban influence, this frozen daiquiri blends rum with the bright citrus flavors of the Florida Keys. Coconut cream, while not classic, adds luscious creaminess. For a traditional take, simply shake and strain the cocktail into a coupe.

---

2 ounces white rum

2 ounces key lime juice, preferably fresh

1 ounce coconut cream

1 ounce Simple Syrup (page 223)

1 cup crushed ice

1 lime wheel, for garnish

In a blender, combine the rum, key lime juice, coconut cream, simple syrup, and crushed ice. Blend until the mixture is smooth. Pour into a rocks or other cocktail glass. Garnish with the lime wheel and serve.

MAKES 1 DRINK

Modern CITRUS DRIFT

Inspired by Florida's rich citrus groves, this modern cocktail highlights the state's vibrant orange industry. Dark rum nods to Florida's Caribbean ties, while Aperol and spiced syrup add depth. Bright, bittersweet, and aromatic, it's a cocktail that captures the essence of Florida's sun-soaked flavors.

- 2 ounces dark rum
- 1 ounce fresh orange juice
- ¾ ounce fresh lime juice
- ½ ounce Aperol
- ½ ounce 5-Spice Simple Syrup (page 223) or Cinnamon-Ginger Simple Syrup (page 223)
- 2 dashes orange bitters
- 1 dehydrated orange wheel, for garnish
- 1 cinnamon stick, for garnish

Fill a cocktail shaker with ice and add the rum, orange juice, lime juice, Aperol, simple syrup, and orange bitters. Cover and shake vigorously until chilled. Strain into a rocks glass over a large ice cube. Garnish with the dehydrated orange wheel and cinnamon stick.

MAKES 1 DRINK

Classic
SCARLETT O'HARA

This classic cocktail, named after the iconic Georgian character from *Gone with the Wind*, blends Southern Comfort, cranberry juice, and lime for a bright, balanced drink. Especially popular in Georgia, its simplicity endures. While the story is rooted in the Civil War and slavery, the cocktail reflects a modern take on the state's complex legacy.

1½ ounces Southern Comfort

1 ounce cranberry juice (not unsweetened)

½ ounce fresh lime juice

1 lime wedge, for garnish

Fill a cocktail shaker with ice and add the Southern Comfort, cranberry juice, and lime juice. Cover and shake vigorously until chilled. Strain into an ice-filled rocks glass. Garnish with the lime wedge and serve.

MAKES 1 DRINK

Modern PEACH STATE PUNCH

Rich with Southern charm, this cocktail blends Georgia's beloved peaches with the warmth of bourbon and the tradition of sweet tea. A touch of basil adds herbal depth, while lemon juice and peach bitters brighten the flavors. Topped with a silky egg-white foam, it's a refined twist on Southern hospitality.

- 2 ounces bourbon
- 1 ounce fresh peach puree or peach juice
- ¾ ounce Sweet Tea–Basil Simple Syrup (page 223)
- ¾ ounce fresh lemon juice
- 2 dashes peach bitters
- ½ ounce egg white
- 1 peach slice, for garnish
- 1 basil leaf, for garnish

Add the bourbon, peach puree, sweet tea–basil syrup, lemon juice, peach bitters, and egg white to a cocktail shaker. Cover and shake vigorously for 30 seconds. Fill the shaker with ice, cover, and continue to shake until well chilled and frothy. Strain into a chilled rocks or coupe glass. Garnish with the peach slice and a smacked basil leaf.

MAKES 1 DRINK

Classic BLUE HAWAII

This vibrant, tropical cocktail was created in 1957 by Harry Yee, the famed bartender at Waikiki's Hilton Hawaiian Village. Tasked with showcasing Bols Blue Curaçao, Yee crafted this eye-catching drink with rum, pineapple juice, and sweet-and-sour mix. Unlike the Blue Hawaiian, which includes coconut cream, the Blue Hawaii is lighter and more citrus-forward, reflecting Hawaii's bright, refreshing flavors. It can also be blended with ice for a frozen version.

---

3 ounces pineapple juice

1½ ounces white rum or vodka (or a mix)

1 ounce Lime Simple Syrup (page 226)

½ ounce blue Curaçao liqueur

1 small pineapple wedge, for garnish

1 cocktail umbrella, for garnish

Fill a cocktail shaker with ice and add the pineapple juice, rum, simple syrup, and blue Curaçao. Cover and shake vigorously until chilled. Fill a hurricane glass with ice cubes or crushed ice. Strain into the glass, garnish with the pineapple wedge and cocktail umbrella, and serve.

MAKES 1 DRINK

Modern
PINEAPPLE GINGER MOJITO

Bright, tropical, and refreshing, this cocktail captures the essence of Hawaii's sun-soaked shores. Sweet island pineapple and zesty ginger blend with fresh mint and lime for a vibrant twist on the classic mojito, celebrating the bold, fresh flavors that make Hawaiian cuisine and cocktails so unforgettable.

- 6 fresh mint leaves
- 2 chunks fresh pineapple
- ½ ounce Ginger Simple Syrup (page 223)
- 2 ounces white rum
- 1 ounce fresh lime juice
- 1 ounce pineapple juice
- 1 ounce club soda
- 1 small fresh pineapple wedge, for garnish
- 1 fresh mint sprig, for garnish

Fill a highball glass with ice. In a cocktail shaker, muddle the mint leaves, fresh pineapple chunks, and ginger syrup. Add ice and then add the rum, lime juice, and pineapple juice. Cover and shake vigorously until chilled. Strain into the ice-filled glass. Top with the club soda and garnish with the pineapple wedge and mint sprig.

MAKES 1 DRINK

Classic
IDAHO SPUD MARTINI

Rooted in Idaho's rich potato heritage, this martini blends potato-based vodka, vermouth, and a dash of celery bitters. Serve alongside a bowl of crisp Idaho potato chips for a cocktail hour that's a savory nod to the Gem State's most famous export.

3 ounces potato-based vodka

½ ounce dry vermouth

2 dashes celery bitters

1 martini olive or cocktail onion, for garnish

In a cocktail shaker filled with ice, combine the vodka, vermouth, and bitters. Cover and shake vigorously until chilled. Strain into a chilled martini glass. Spear the olive or onion with a cocktail pick and garnish the martini with it. Serve with a bowl of potato chips.

MAKES 1 DRINK

Modern SNAKE RIVER SOUR

Inspired by Idaho's wild beauty, this modern sour blends whiskey, lemon juice, egg white, and huckleberry syrup—an ode to the tart berries native to the state and found in abundance across its mountains and forests. The Snake River winds through the heart of Idaho, carving canyons and nourishing valleys where wild huckleberries thrive—lending both its name and untamed spirit to this vibrant cocktail.

---

2 ounces whiskey

¾ ounce fresh lemon juice

½ ounce huckleberry simple syrup (page 226), plus more for garnish

2 or 3 dashes Angostura bitters, plus more for garnish

½ ounce egg white

Add the whiskey, lemon juice, simple syrup, bitters, and egg white to a cocktail shaker. Cover and shake vigorously for 30 seconds. Fill the shaker with ice, cover, and continue to shake until well chilled and frothy. Strain into a chilled rocks or coupe glass. Garnish with a few drops of the bitters and/or the syrup. Serve.

MAKES 1 DRINK

Classic CHICAGO FIZZ

A stylish, spirited classic, this cocktail blends dark rum and ruby port with lemon and egg white to create a rich, frothy cocktail. Though its origins in the Windy City are hazy, it gained national attention pre-Prohibition and was once served at the Waldorf Astoria before fading nearly into obscurity.

- 1½ ounces dark rum
- 1½ ounces ruby port
- ¾ ounce fresh lemon juice
- ½ ounce Simple Syrup (page 223)
- ½ ounce egg white
- 2 ounces club soda
- 1 lemon wedge, for garnish

Add the rum, port, lemon juice, syrup, and egg white to a cocktail shaker. Cover and shake vigorously for 30 seconds. Fill the shaker with ice, cover, and continue to shake until well chilled and frothy. Strain into a chilled, ice-filled collins glass. Top with club soda, garnish with a lemon wedge, and serve.

MAKES 1 DRINK

Modern PRAIRIE SMASH

This refreshing, updated cocktail blends whiskey with fresh strawberries and basil, both key crops in Illinois, where the state's rich farmland nurtures their growth. Rhubarb bitters add a tart twist, while honey simple syrup highlights Illinois' thriving beekeeping industry. Together, these ingredients capture the essence of the state's seasonal harvests and its abundant agricultural landscape.

- 2 ripe strawberries, hulled
- 4 fresh basil leaves
- 2 ounces whiskey, bourbon, or rye
- ¾ ounce fresh lemon juice
- ½ ounce Honey Simple Syrup (page 224)
- 2 dashes rhubarb bitters
- 2 ounces club soda
- 1 small basil sprig, for garnish

Fill a rocks or highball glass with ice. In a cocktail shaker, muddle the strawberries and basil leaves together. Add ice and then add the whiskey, lemon juice, simple syrup, and rhubarb bitters. Cover and shake vigorously until chilled. Strain into the ice-filled glass. Top with the club soda and garnish with the basil sprig. Serve.

MAKES 1 DRINK

Classic HOOSIER HERITAGE

This unofficial state cocktail—originally created by Jason Foust for the 2015 Indiana State Museum's Making Indiana's Cocktail Contest—blends rye whiskey, apple cider, lemon juice, and maple syrup, each ingredient reflecting Indiana's evolving agricultural heritage. While the state's maple syrup production remains modest, it's growing steadily, just like Indiana's whiskey industry. With producers like Ross & Squibb Distillery in Lawrenceburg fueling a national rye resurgence, this cocktail is a spirited blending of both tradition and innovation.

- 1 tablespoon fresh rosemary leaves
- ½ ounce maple syrup
- 2 ounces rye whiskey
- 1 ounce apple cider
- ½ ounce fresh lemon juice
- 1 small rosemary sprig, for garnish
- 1 thin apple slice, for garnish

Fill a rocks glass with ice. In a cocktail shaker, muddle the rosemary leaves and maple syrup together. Add ice and then add the whiskey, apple cider, and lemon juice. Cover and shake vigorously until chilled. Strain into the ice-filled glass. Garnish with the rosemary sprig and apple slice. Serve.

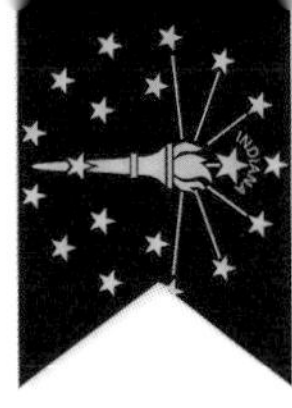

MAKES 1 DRINK

Modern PERSIMMON HARVEST

This modern cocktail showcases Indiana's native American persimmon (Diospyros virginiana), prized for its rich, honeyed flavor and custard-like texture when fully ripe. Hachiya persimmon makes a fine substitute. Blended with Indiana bourbon, maple, lemon, and cinnamon-ginger syrup, it's a silky, spiced tribute to the Midwest's late-autumn harvest.

- 2 ounces bourbon
- 1 ounce American persimmon puree (or Hachiya persimmon if unavailable)
- ½ ounce Cinnamon-Ginger Simple Syrup (page 223)
- ½ ounce fresh lemon juice
- ¼ ounce maple syrup
- Freshly grated cinnamon, for garnish
- 1 dehydrated persimmon slice, for garnish

In a cocktail shaker filled with ice, combine the bourbon, persimmon puree, simple syrup, lemon juice, and maple syrup. Cover and shake vigorously until chilled. Strain into an ice-filled rocks glass. Garnish with the cinnamon and dehydrated persimmon slice. Serve.

MAKES 1 DRINK

Classic IOWA MULE

This refreshing mule combines corn whiskey, lime juice, and ginger beer, capturing the essence of Iowa's agricultural roots. With corn as the state's top crop, local distilleries like Century Farms and Iowa Distilling Company craft unique corn whiskeys, showcasing Iowa's deep connection to this iconic American spirit in every sip.

- 2 ounces corn whiskey
- 1 ounce fresh lime juice
- 4 to 6 ounces ginger beer
- 1 lime wedge, for garnish

Fill a copper mug or rocks glass with ice. Add the whiskey, lime juice, and ginger beer and stir gently. Garnish with the lime wedge and serve.

MAKES 1 DRINK

Modern CORNFIELD SOUR

This cocktail celebrates Iowa's thriving corn industry, using corn whiskey—preferably from one of the state's celebrated distilleries—and fresh corn puree to create a bold, unexpected flavor profile. The earthy sweetness of the corn is complemented by honey syrup and fresh lemon juice, while the charred corn husk garnish adds a smoky, modern twist.

- 1 tablespoon fresh (or thawed frozen) corn kernels
- ¾ ounce fresh lemon juice
- 2 ounces corn whiskey or bourbon
- ½ ounce Honey Simple Syrup (page 224)
- ½ ounce egg white
- 1 piece corn husk, for garnish

In a cocktail shaker, muddle the corn kernels and lemon juice together. Add the whiskey, simple syrup, and egg white to the shaker. Cover and shake vigorously for 30 seconds. Fill the shaker with ice, cover, and continue to shake until well chilled and frothy. Strain into a chilled, ice-filled rocks glass. Light a match and use the flame to char the corn husk. Drop the charred husk into the drink to garnish and serve.

MAKES 1 DRINK

Classic HORSEFEATHER

A spicy, citrusy staple with Midwestern roots, this bold blend of rye whiskey, ginger beer, bitters, and lemon delivers a refreshing kick. Popular in Kansas City, its origins are often traced to Lawrence, Kansas, cementing its place in the Sunflower State's cocktail canon.

---

2 ounces rye whiskey
1 ounce lemon juice
3 dashes Angostura bitters
3 to 4 ounces ginger beer
1 mint leaf, for garnish

Combine the whiskey, lemon juice, and bitters in a highball glass. Add ice and stir well. Top with the ginger beer. Garnish with a mint leaf and serve.

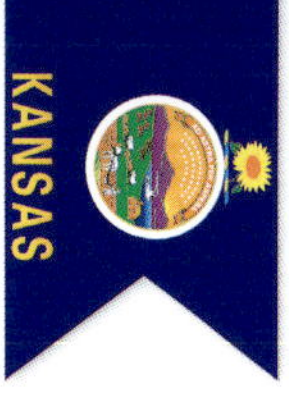

MAKES 1 DRINK

Modern KANSAS CHERRY NEGRONI

A modern Kansas twist on the classic Negroni, this bold cocktail blends wheat whiskey, sour cherries, and Campari for a tangy-bitter bite. With Kansas leading the nation in wheat production and rich in sour cherries, this drink is a spirited tribute to the heartland's agricultural bounty and creative flair. For a smoky finish, smoke the rocks glass as instructed on page 19.

6 pitted sour cherries

1 ounce wheat-based whiskey

1 ounce sweet vermouth

½ ounce Campari

½ ounce tart cherry simple syrup (page 226)

2 dashes orange bitters

1 fresh sour cherry with stem and/or 1 orange peel twist, for garnish

In a cocktail shaker, muddle the sour cherries. Add ice and then add the whiskey, vermouth, Campari, simple syrup, and orange bitters. Cover and shake vigorously until chilled. Add a large ice cube to a rocks glass. Strain the cocktail into the ice-filled glass. Garnish with the sour cherry and/or orange peel twist and serve.

MAKES 1 DRINK

Classic MINT JULEP

Rooted in Kentucky tradition, the mint julep is a timeless blend of bourbon, fresh mint, sugar, and crushed ice. Popularized at the Kentucky Derby and deeply tied to the state's bourbon heritage, this refreshing sipper has been a Southern staple since the eighteenth century—cool, crisp, and unmistakably Kentucky.

- 9 fresh mint leaves
- 1 ounce mint simple syrup
- 2 ounces bourbon
- 1 ounce fresh lime juice
- 1 lime wedge, for garnish

In a rocks glass, muddle 8 of the mint leaves and the simple syrup. Add the bourbon and lime juice, pack the glass tightly with crushed ice, and stir until the glass is frosted on the outside. Top with more crushed ice to form a dome. Garnish with the remaining mint leaf and the lime wedge and serve.

MAKES 1 DRINK

Modern KENTUCKY BLUEGRASS SMASH

A vibrant tribute to the Bluegrass State, this modern bourbon smash blends blackberry-mint syrup, elderflower liqueur, fresh lime, and a splash of club soda. With deep roots in Kentucky's bourbon legacy and abundant summer berries, it's a fresh, floral take that captures the spirit—and sweetness—of Southern hospitality.

- 5 fresh blackberries
- ¾ ounce Blackberry-Mint Simple Syrup (page 226)
- 2 ounces bourbon
- ½ ounce fresh lime juice
- ½ ounce elderflower liqueur, preferably St-Germain
- 1 ounce club soda (or to taste)
- 1 mint sprig, for garnish
- Grated lime zest, for garnish

Fill a rocks glass with ice. In a cocktail shaker, muddle 4 of the blackberries and the simple syrup. Add ice and then add the bourbon, lime juice, and elderflower liqueur. Cover and shake vigorously until chilled. Strain into the ice-filled glass. Top with club soda. Garnish with the remaining blackberry, the mint sprig, and grated lime zest. Serve.

MAKES 1 DRINK

Classic SAZERAC

A New Orleans icon, this cousin of the old-fashioned blends rye whiskey (or brandy), bitters, sugar, and absinthe for a bold, aromatic sip. First mixed in the 1800s with French cognac, the Sazerac has deep roots in the Crescent City—officially crowned in 2008 but revered long before that.

- ¼ ounce absinthe
- 1 sugar cube
- 3 dashes Peychaud's bitters
- 1 dash Angostura bitters (optional)
- ¼ ounce water
- 2½ ounces rye whiskey
- 1 lemon twist, for garnish

Pour the absinthe into a rocks glass and swirl to coat the sides. Add 1 large ice cube; set aside.

In a cocktail shaker, muddle the sugar cube, Peychaud's bitters, Angostura bitters (if using), and water. Fill the shaker with ice and add the rye whiskey. Cover and shake vigorously until chilled. Discard the ice and any excess absinthe from the prepared rocks glass. Strain the contents of the cocktail shaker into the glass. Twist the lemon over the surface of the cocktail to express the citrus oil, then garnish with the lemon twist and serve.

MAKES 1 DRINK

Modern TROPICAL FIZZ

A bright, modern take on the classic New Orleans hurricane, this tropical sipper swaps sugary punch for balance and fizz. With dark rum, passion fruit puree, lime, ginger syrup, and sparkling water, the Tropical Fizz offers a fresh, refined update—still bold and festive, but with a lighter, contemporary twist.

- 2 ounces dark or white rum
- 1 ounce Pineapple-Pomegranate Shrub (page 229)
- 1 ounce pineapple juice
- ¾ ounce passion fruit puree
- ¾ ounce fresh lime juice
- 1 ounce sparkling water
- 1 dehydrated lime wheel, for garnish
- 1 small mint sprig, for garnish

In a cocktail shaker filled with ice, combine the rum, pineapple-pomegranate shrub, pineapple juice, passion fruit puree, and lime juice. Cover and shake vigorously until chilled. Strain into an ice-filled hurricane or other tall glass. Top with sparkling water. Garnish with the lime wheel and mint sprig. Serve.

MAKES 1 DRINK

Classic LOBSTER BLOODY MARY

Brimming with coastal character, this bold drink channels the essence of Maine. Spiked with zesty lemon, horseradish, and a dash of brine, it's finished with sweet lobster meat—a nod to the state's seafood legacy. Ideal for seaside brunches or for bringing a taste of the Atlantic to your table.

---

1 teaspoon Old Bay Seasoning, for rimming the glass

1 lemon wedge

4 ounces tomato juice

2 ounces vodka

1 ounce fresh lemon juice

½ ounce pickle juice

½ teaspoon prepared horseradish

½ teaspoon Worcestershire sauce

2 dashes Tabasco or other hot pepper sauce

Freshly ground white pepper

Cooked lobster meat, pitted green olives, celery stalk, and pickle spear, for garnish

---

Pour the Old Bay Seasoning onto a small plate. Gently rub the lemon wedge around the rim of a pint glass. Holding the base of the glass, dip the rim into the seasoning.

Fill a cocktail shaker half full of ice. Add the tomato juice, vodka, lemon juice, pickle juice, horseradish, Worcestershire, Tabasco, and a pinch of white pepper. Cover and shake vigorously until chilled. Strain into the glass. Add ice.

Spear the lobster meat and olives with a long cocktail pick and balance over the top of the glass. Add a celery stalk and pickle spear and serve.

MAKES 1 DRINK

Modern WILD BLUEBERRY HIGHBALL

This refreshing highball is a tribute to Maine's wild blueberries and quirky charm. Blueberry-infused gin and syrup meet the bold bite of Moxie—Maine's iconic soda—for a cocktail that's equal parts nostalgic and new. Finished with citrus bitters and a twist of orange, it's summer in the pines, bottled.

---

2 ounces blueberry-infused gin (see Note)

½ ounce wild blueberry simple syrup (page 226)

2 dashes orange or other citrus bitters

3 ounces Moxie soda

1 orange peel twist, for garnish

3 skewered blueberries, for garnish

In a cocktail shaker filled with ice, combine the gin, simple syrup, and bitters. Cover and shake vigorously until chilled. Strain into an ice-filled highball glass. Top with Moxie soda. Garnish with the orange twist and blueberry skewer. Serve.

NOTE

To make blueberry-infused gin, start by placing ½ cup of fresh blueberries in a clean jar or bottle. Pour 1 cup of gin over the blueberries, ensuring they are fully covered. Seal the container and store it in a cool, dark place for 3 to 5 days, gently shaking the jar once a day. Once the gin has taken on a vibrant color and fruity flavor, strain out the blueberries and transfer the infused gin to a clean bottle or jar. Store it in the refrigerator.

MAKES 1 DRINK

Classic BLACK-EYED SUSAN

Named for Maryland's state flower and served at the iconic Preakness Stakes, the black-eyed Susan is a zesty, sun-kissed cocktail. With vodka, bourbon or rum, and plenty of citrus and tropical fruit flavors, it channels the energy of race day at Pimlico and the bold, breezy charm of the Old Line State.

---

1 ounce vodka

1 ounce bourbon or white rum

1 ounce fresh orange juice

1 ounce pineapple juice

½ ounce orange liqueur

½ ounce Lemon-Lime Simple Syrup (page 227) or sour mix

1 orange slice, for garnish

1 lime wheel, for garnish

1 maraschino cherry, for garnish

Fill a cocktail shaker with ice. Add the vodka, bourbon, orange juice, pineapple juice, orange liqueur, and simple syrup. Shake well until chilled. Strain into an ice-filled highball or collins glass. Garnish with the orange slice, lime wheel, and cherry. Serve.

MAKES 1 DRINK

Modern CHESAPEAKE EMBER

Rich with Maryland traditions, this contemporary cocktail blends bold rye whiskey—a spirit with deep roots in the state—with molasses, a Chesapeake staple shaped by a complex history of trade. Spices such as star anise and pepper, once carried through Baltimore's busy port, meet dark cherry liqueur in a nod to the region's wild fruits and lush summers.

Smoked salt, for rimming the glass

2 ounces rye whiskey, preferably Maryland-style

½ ounce Spiced Molasses Simple Syrup (page 224)

½ ounce dark cherry liqueur, such as Heering

2 dashes orange bitters

1 cocktail cherry, for garnish

Rim a chilled rocks glass with smoked salt and add 1 large ice cube.

Fill a cocktail shaker with ice. Add the rye, simple syrup, cherry liqueur, and bitters. Shake well until chilled. Strain into the prepared glass. Garnish with the cherry and serve.

MAKES 1 DRINK

Classic CAPE CODDER

Bright and refreshing, the Cape Codder captures the spirit of coastal Massachusetts. Named for the state's iconic peninsula, this simple mix of vodka and cranberry juice pays tribute to the region's historic cranberry bogs. A squeeze of fresh lime adds a crisp finish to this easy-drinking New England classic.

- 2 ounces vodka
- 4 ounces cranberry juice
- 1 lime wedge, for garnish

Fill a highball glass with ice. Add the vodka and cranberry juice and stir gently to combine. Garnish with a lime wedge, squeezing the lime over the drink for extra brightness, and serve.

MAKES 1 DRINK

Modern BOSTON BOULEVARDIER

This cocktail cousin of the Negroni reimagines the classic with rye whiskey, mead or apple vermouth, and a bittersweet kick of Campari. Local ties shine through in the use of mead and apple, staples of Massachusetts agriculture, while a flamed orange peel and infused cherry add bold, modern character to the drink.

- 1 ounce rye whiskey
- 1 ounce mead, apple vermouth, or sweet vermouth
- ½ ounce Campari
- 2 dashes orange bitters
- 1 cocktail cherry, for garnish
- 1 orange peel, made with a vegetable peeler

Fill a cocktail shaker with ice. Add the rye whiskey, mead or vermouth, Campari, and orange bitters and shake to combine. Strain into an ice-filled rocks glass. Garnish with the cherry. Light a match, then twist and squeeze the orange peel over the flame. Rub the peel around the rim of the glass, drop it into the drink, and serve.

MAKES 1 DRINK

Classic HUMMER

Invented in 1968 by Detroit bartender Jerome Adams at the Bayview Yacht Club, the Hummer quickly became a Michigan classic. Thick, creamy, and tasting like coffee ice cream, this blend of rum, Kahlúa, and vanilla ice cream captured the spirit of Detroit's sailing scene and spread across the state.

- 1½ ounces white rum
- 1½ ounces Kahlúa or crème de cacao
- 2 scoops vanilla ice cream
- ½ cup crushed ice

Add the rum, Kahlúa, ice cream, and crushed ice to a blender and blend on medium-high speed until smooth. Pour into a chilled rocks glass or highball glass and serve.

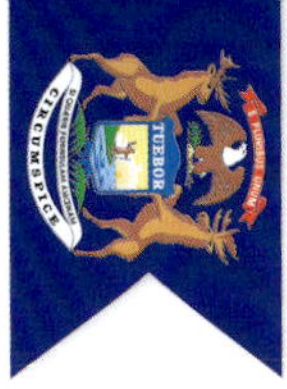

MAKES 1 DRINK

Modern CHERRY SPARK

Michigan's bright, tart Montmorency cherries shine alongside local rye or bourbon in this lively, layered cocktail. A splash of Vernors—the state's iconic ginger soda—adds crisp sweetness, while fresh rosemary and herbal bitters evoke the woodsy freshness of Michigan's orchards and fields.

---

7 pitted fresh sour cherries, preferably Montmorency

2 small fresh rosemary sprigs

½ ounce cherry liqueur, such as Heering

2 ounces rye whiskey or bourbon, preferably from Michigan

2 dashes Angostura bitters

2 ounces Vernors Ginger Soda or ginger beer

1 orange peel, made with a vegetable peeler

In a cocktail shaker, muddle together 6 of the pitted sour cherries, 1 of the rosemary sprigs, and the cherry liqueur. Fill the shaker with ice and add the rye whiskey and bitters. Cover and shake vigorously until chilled. Strain into a chilled coupe glass. Top with the ginger soda.

Light a match, then twist and squeeze the orange peel over the flame. Rub the peel along the rim of the glass. Spear the remaining cherry and the orange peel on a cocktail pick and add them to the drink along with the remaining rosemary sprig for garnish. Serve.

MAKES 1 DRINK

Classic
THE BOOTLEG

In Minnesota, Memorial Day marks the unofficial start of Bootleg season. Born during Prohibition on Lake Minnetonka, this minty, citrusy cooler became a lakeside staple, masking spirits behind fresh flavors. Twin Cities country clubs fiercely claim its invention, making it as much a part of Minnesota summers as boating and bonfires.

- 6 to 8 fresh mint leaves
- ¾ ounce fresh lemon juice
- ¾ ounce fresh lime juice
- ¾ ounce Simple Syrup (page 223)
- 2 ounces gin or vodka
- 2 ounces club soda
- 1 small fresh mint sprig, for garnish

In a cocktail shaker, muddle together the mint leaves, lemon and lime juices, and the simple syrup. Fill the shaker with ice and add the gin. Cover and shake vigorously until chilled. Strain into a chilled, ice-filled highball glass. Top with the club soda. Garnish with the mint sprig and serve.

MAKES 1 DRINK

Modern BOTANICAL BLISS

Drawing inspiration from Minnesota's rich gardens and fields, this fresh cocktail blends juicy native blueberries, cooling cucumber, and delicate lemon balm. Chamomile syrup adds a soft floral touch, in a nod to the wildflowers that brighten the state's landscapes each summer. It's a refreshing, deeply local taste of a northern growing season.

- 8 fresh blueberries
- 4 lemon balm leaves or mint leaves
- 3 thin cucumber slices
- 2 ounces gin
- ¾ ounce Chamomile Simple Syrup (page 223)
- ¾ ounce fresh lime juice
- 2 ounces club soda
- 1 cucumber ribbon speared on a cocktail pick, for garnish

In a cocktail shaker, muddle together the blueberries, lemon balm leaves, and cucumber slices. Fill the shaker with ice and add the gin, simple syrup, and lime juice. Cover and shake vigorously until chilled. Strain the contents of the shaker into a chilled highball glass. Top with the club soda. Garnish with the speared cucumber ribbon and serve.

MAKES 1 DRINK

Classic MISSISSIPPI PUNCH

First recorded in Jerry Thomas's 1862 *How to Mix Drinks*, Mississippi punch blends cognac, bourbon, rum, lemon, and sugar into a bold, spirited mix. Reflecting the diverse influences along the Mississippi River, this lively, potent punch captures the hospitality, complexity, and rich cultural currents of the South in one timeless glass.

---

2 ounces cognac or brandy

1 ounce bourbon

½ ounce dark rum

1 ounce fresh lemon juice

1 ounce fresh orange juice

1 ounce Honey Simple Syrup (page 224)

1 lemon wheel, for garnish

Fill a cocktail shaker with ice. Add the cognac, bourbon, rum, lemon and orange juices, and simple syrup. Cover and shake vigorously until chilled. Strain into an ice-filled collins or highball glass. Garnish with the lemon wheel and serve.

MAKES 1 DRINK

Modern SOUTHERN BLACKBERRY COLLINS

Mississippi's wild blackberries take center stage in this contemporary twist on a collins. Infused with thyme for a fresh, herbal edge and paired with citrusy brightness from lemon and orange bitters, this drink is light yet complex. Topped with a fresh blackberry garnish, it's a crisp, vibrant taste of the season.

1½ ounces gin

½ ounce fresh lemon juice

¾ ounce Blackberry-Thyme Simple Syrup (page 226)

2 or 3 dashes orange bitters

5 to 6 ounces club soda

1 lemon twist, for garnish

3 fresh blackberries, speared, for garnish

Fill a cocktail shaker with ice. Add the gin, lemon juice, simple syrup, and bitters. Cover and shake vigorously until chilled. Strain into an ice-filled collins glass. Top with the club soda and stir. Garnish with the lemon twist and blackberries. Serve.

MAKES 1 DRINK

Classic
MISSOURI MULE

A twist on the Moscow mule, this drink combines Missouri's rich bourbon heritage with local apple brandy in recognition of the state's abundant orchards. Campari adds depth, while Cointreau introduces a citrusy finish. Served in a copper mug, it's a refreshing taste of Missouri craftsmanship and flavor.

1½ ounces bourbon, preferably from Missouri

¾ ounce apple brandy

½ ounce Campari

½ ounce orange liqueur, such as Cointreau

2 ounces ginger beer or club soda

1 thin orange slice, for garnish

2 thin apple slices, for garnish

Fill a copper mug or rocks glass with ice. Add the bourbon, apple brandy, Campari, and orange liqueur and stir. Top with ginger beer. Garnish with the orange and apple slices and serve.

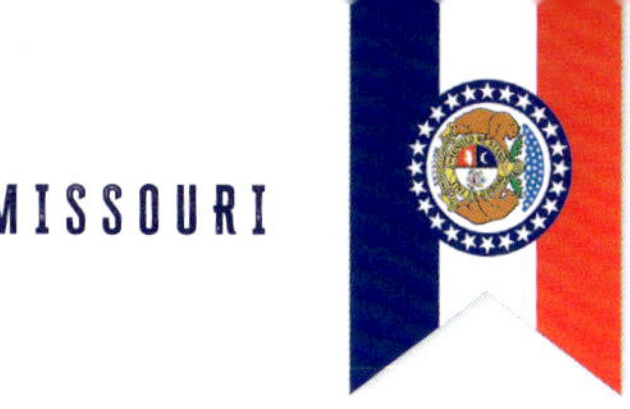

MAKES 1 DRINK

Modern
RIVER CITY REFRESHER

This modern cocktail blends Missouri's agricultural bounty with St. Louis's vibrant craft-cocktail culture. Blackberry-infused vodka and apple shrub showcase local fruits, while ginger kombucha and bitters add bite. Garnished with blackberries, it's a zingy, effervescent celebration of the state's flavors.

- 2 ounces blackberry-infused vodka (see Note)
- 1½ ounces Apple Shrub (page 229)
- 3 dashes ginger bitters
- 3 ounces ginger kombucha
- 1 thin apple slice, for garnish
- 3 fresh blackberries, speared, for garnish

In a cocktail shaker filled with ice, combine the vodka, apple shrub, and bitters. Cover and shake vigorously until chilled. Strain into an ice-filled rocks glass. Top with the kombucha and stir gently. Garnish with the apple slice and blackberries and serve.

NOTE

To make homemade blackberry-infused vodka, combine ½ cup fresh blackberries with 1 cup vodka in a clean jar. If you prefer a touch of sweetness, you can add about 1 teaspoon sugar and stir gently. Seal the jar and store it in a cool, dark place for 3 to 5 days, giving the mixture a gentle shake each day. Once the vodka has taken on a rich berry flavor and color, strain out the blackberries using a fine mesh strainer or cheesecloth. Transfer the infused vodka to a clean bottle or jar and keep it in the refrigerator.

MAKES 1 DRINK

Classic

THE MONTANA MARTINI

A tribute to Harry Johnson's 1900 Montana cocktail, the Montana martini preserves its sloe gin and dry vermouth core while streamlining ingredients. Anisette gives way to absinthe, Boker's bitters to orange, and a citrus twist brightens the finish. It's a crisp, aromatic revival of a nearly forgotten classic.

2 ounces sloe gin

1 ounce dry vermouth

Dash of absinthe

Dash of orange bitters

1 orange twist, for garnish

In a cocktail shaker filled with ice, combine the sloe gin, vermouth, absinthe, and orange bitters. Cover and shake vigorously until chilled. Strain into a chilled martini glass. Garnish with the orange twist and serve.

MAKES 1 DRINK

Modern
THE MOUNTAIN BREEZE

This modern cocktail celebrates Montana's wild ingredients, featuring saskatoon berries—a local fruit with sweet, earthy flavors—and juniper berries, which grow across the state's rugged landscapes and are a key ingredient in Montana-made gin. Paired with fresh herbs such as rosemary, thyme, and lemon balm, it's a balanced botanical drink that captures the state's natural beauty. Look for saskatoon syrup in local shops or online.

---

1 tablespoon mixed fresh herb leaves, such as rosemary, thyme, and lemon balm

¾ ounce saskatoon berry syrup

½ ounce fresh lime juice

1¾ ounces gin, preferably from Montana and infused with juniper berries

2 ounces club soda

1 small juniper sprig or other herb sprig, for garnish

In a cocktail shaker, muddle together the herbs, saskatoon berry syrup, and lime juice. Fill the shaker with ice and add the gin. Cover and shake vigorously until chilled. Strain into a chilled highball or collins glass. Add ice, then top with the club soda. Garnish with the juniper sprig and serve.

MAKES 1 DRINK

Classic RED BEER

This refreshing drink, a favorite at brunches and tailgates across Nebraska, combines tomato juice, beer, and lime with a Tajín rim for an added kick. Similar to a michelada, it's as much a regional tradition as it is a satisfying hangover cure, embodying the heartland's love for easygoing drinks.

- 3 lime wedges
- 1 teaspoon Tajín seasoning, for rimming the glass
- 3 ounces tomato juice
- 6 to 8 ounces lager-style or light beer

Rub the rim of a chilled pint glass with 1 of the lime wedges. Spread the Tajín seasoning on a saucer and dip the rim of the glass in the seasoning to coat the edges. Fill the glass two-thirds full of ice.

Pour the tomato juice into the glass. Squeeze 1 lime wedge into the tomato juice, then drop it in. Top with beer and stir gently. Garnish with the remaining lime wedge on the rim and serve.

MAKES 1 DRINK

Modern SUNFLOWER SPRITZ

This bright spritz captures Nebraska's agricultural spirit. Corn-based vodka reflects the state's farming pride, while black chokeberries—native fruits traditionally used by Indigenous peoples—add tart depth. A homemade sunflower seed orgeat lends nutty richness, and a splash of club soda gives it sparkle, bringing all the ingredients together in a lively tribute to the Great Plains. Aronia berry syrup can be purchased in local shops or online.

2 ounces corn vodka, preferably from Nebraska

¾ ounce aronia (chokeberry) syrup or blackberry simple syrup (page 226)

½ ounce Sunflower Seed Orgeat (page 223) or almond orgeat

½ ounce fresh lemon juice

1 ounce club soda

Food-grade sunflower petals, for garnish

In a cocktail shaker filled with ice, combine the vodka, aronia syrup, sunflower seed orgeat, and lemon juice. Cover and shake vigorously until chilled. Strain into a chilled coupe glass. Top with the club soda and stir gently. Garnish with a few fresh sunflower petals floated on top and serve.

MAKES 1 DRINK

Classic PICON PUNCH

Brought to Nevada by Basque immigrants, this bold cocktail became a mainstay of the state's boardinghouses and restaurants. Mixing bitter Amer Picon, grenadine, brandy, and club soda, it embodies Nevada's Basque-American heritage. Officially named the state cocktail in 2023, it remains a vibrant symbol of tradition and community in Nevada.

- ¼ ounce grenadine
- 2 ounces Amer Picon, Ferino Amer, or Torani Amer
- ½ ounce brandy
- ¼ ounce fresh lemon juice
- 2 ounces club soda
- 1 lemon twist, for garnish

In an ice-filled rocks glass, add the grenadine. Pour in the Amer Picon, then the brandy and lemon juice. Stir gently with a bar spoon, top with the club soda, stir again, and then squeeze a lemon twist over the drink and rub it around the rim. Drop the twist into the cocktail and serve.

MAKES 1 DRINK

Modern
DESERT DUNE RIDER

Inspired by Nevada's rugged desert landscapes, this refreshing cocktail highlights ingredients rooted in the region. Floral desert honey and wild sage evoke the state's arid beauty, while bright citrus and crisp Topo Chico add lift. It's a refreshing, earthy drink that captures the spirit of Nevada's open spaces.

---

1 lime wedge

1 teaspoon smoked salt or kosher salt, for rimming the glass

¼ teaspoon ground sage, for rimming the glass

2 ounces blanco or reposado tequila

1 ounce fresh grapefruit juice

½ ounce fresh lime juice

¾ ounce Honey-Sage Simple Syrup (page 224), preferably made with Nevada desert honey

2 ounces sparkling water, preferably Topo Chico

1 fresh sage leaf, for garnish

Rub the rim of a chilled rocks glass or highball glass with the lime wedge. Combine the smoked salt and sage on a saucer and dip the rim of the glass in the seasoning to coat the edges. Fill the glass with ice.

In a shaker filled with ice, combine the tequila, grapefruit juice, lime juice, and simple syrup. Cover and shake vigorously until well chilled. Strain into the prepared glass.

Top with sparkling water and stir gently. Light a match, then twist and squeeze the sage leaf over the flame. Drop the leaf into the drink and serve.

MAKES 1 DRINK

Classic SPIKED APPLE CIDER

New Hampshire's crisp autumns and abundant apple orchards inspire this cozy cocktail. Fresh apple cider, apple brandy, and a hint of maple—inspired by the state's rich syrup tradition—come together with a splash of lemon for brightness. It's a warm, comforting drink that captures classic New England flavors. Try it chilled over ice for a warm-weather refresher too. You can multiply this by four to make a bigger batch to share.

- 6 ounces fresh apple cider
- ½ cinnamon stick
- ½ star anise (optional)
- 2 ounces apple brandy
- ½ ounce maple syrup
- ¼ ounce fresh lemon juice
- 1 thin apple slice, for garnish

In a small saucepan over low heat, warm the apple cider, cinnamon stick, and star anise (if using) just until the cider is steaming; do not boil. Pour into a mug and add the apple brandy, maple syrup, and lemon juice. Stir to combine. Garnish with the apple slice and serve.

MAKES 1 DRINK

Modern WHITE MOUNTAIN REFRESHER

Named for New Hampshire's famous White Mountains, this bright, herbaceous cocktail captures the state's natural beauty. Botanical gin, black-currant liqueur, and lemon balm syrup highlight New England's wild fruits and herbs, while cold-brew green tea adds refreshing depth. A garnish of pine or a sprig of lemon balm completes this alpine-inspired drink.

- 1½ ounces gin
- ½ ounce black-currant liqueur, such as crème de cassis
- ½ ounce Lemon Balm Simple Syrup (page 223)
- 3 ounces unsweetened cold-brew green tea
- 1 small pine frond or 1 small sprig lemon balm, for garnish

In a cocktail shaker filled with ice, combine the gin, black-currant liqueur, simple syrup, and green tea. Cover and shake vigorously until well chilled. Strain into an ice-filled rocks glass. Garnish with the pine frond and serve.

MAKES 1 DRINK

Classic JACK ROSE

Though its exact origins are unclear, this classic cocktail likely ties back to New Jersey, thanks to its base spirit, Laird's Applejack—made at the nation's oldest licensed distillery. Popular through Prohibition and famously favored by Steinbeck and Hemingway, the Jack Rose remains a timeless tribute to American apple brandy.

---

2 ounces applejack or apple brandy

¾ ounce fresh lemon or lime juice

½ ounce grenadine

1 lemon twist, for garnish

In a cocktail shaker filled with ice, combine the applejack, lemon juice, and grenadine. Cover and shake vigorously until well chilled. Strain into a chilled coupe glass. Garnish with the lemon twist and serve.

MAKES 1 DRINK

Modern GARDEN STATE FIZZ

Celebrating New Jersey's agricultural heritage, this bright, refreshing cocktail features tart cranberry shrub—an homage to the state's historic cranberry bogs—and garden-fresh basil and mint. Paired with craft gin and a lively splash of tonic or sparkling wine, it's a crisp, vibrant tribute to the Garden State's bounty.

- 1½ ounces craft gin, preferably from New Jersey
- 1 ounce Cranberry Shrub (page 227)
- ¾ ounce fresh lime juice
- ½ ounce Basil-Mint Simple Syrup (page 223)
- ½ ounce egg white
- 1 ounce club soda or lime sparkling water
- 1 small fresh basil or mint sprig, for garnish

In a cocktail shaker, combine the gin, cranberry shrub, lime juice, simple syrup, and egg white. Cover and shake vigorously for 30 seconds. Fill the shaker with ice, cover, and continue to shake until well chilled and frothy. Strain into an ice-filled rocks glass. Top with the club soda. Garnish with the basil sprig and serve.

MAKES 1 DRINK

Classic CHIMAYÓ COCKTAIL

Rooted in the orchards of Chimayo, New Mexico, this cocktail blends crisp apple cider with smooth tequila and a hint of black currant. Created at the restaurant Rancho de Chimayó in the 1960s, it captures the unique agricultural bounty of northern New Mexico in a light, slightly earthy drink with rich local ties. For a refreshing variation, top the cocktail with ginger beer.

---

2 ounces blanco or reposado tequila

2 ounces fresh apple cider

1 ounce black-currant liqueur, such as crème de cassis

½ ounce fresh lemon juice

1 thin apple slice or lemon wheel

In a cocktail shaker filled with ice, combine the tequila, apple cider, crème de cassis, and lemon juice. Cover and shake vigorously until well chilled. Strain into an ice-filled collins glass. Garnish with the apple slice or lemon wheel and serve.

MAKES 1 DRINK

Modern DESERT BLOOM

Inspired by New Mexico's vibrant landscapes, this cocktail layers smoky mezcal, tart hibiscus, and the heat of local chiles. Lavender and honey, both abundant in the high desert, add a floral sweetness, while grapefruit brings a refreshing brightness. It's a vivid, desert-born drink that blooms with the spirit of the Southwest.

---

1 ounce fresh grapefruit juice

1 teaspoon dried chile salt, for rimming the glass

1½ ounces mezcal

2 ounces brewed and cooled hibiscus tea

½ ounce Lavender-Chile Honey Simple Syrup (page 224)

2 ounces sparkling water

1 small sprig of desert lavender, for garnish

Rub the rim of a chilled collins or highball glass with a little grapefruit juice. Spread the chile salt on a saucer and dip the rim of the glass in the seasoning to coat the edges. Fill the glass with ice.

In a cocktail shaker filled with ice, combine the mezcal, tea, the remaining grapefruit juice, and simple syrup. Cover and shake vigorously until well chilled. Strain into the prepared glass. Top with the sparkling water. Garnish with the lavender sprig and serve.

MAKES 1 DRINK

Classic MANHATTAN

The Manhattan first appeared in the 1870s, likely at a New York City bar rather than the famed Manhattan Club, despite popular legend. Blending American rye whiskey, sweet vermouth, and bitters, the cocktail captured the city's energy—elegant yet strong—and quickly became a fixture of New York's golden age of cocktails.

---

2 ounces rye whiskey

1 ounce sweet vermouth

2 dashes Angostura or orange bitters

1 premium cocktail cherry in syrup

Half-fill a cocktail shaker with ice. Add the rye whiskey, vermouth, and bitters and, using a bar spoon, stir well. Strain into a chilled coupe glass. Garnish with the cherry and serve.

MAKES 1 DRINK

Modern COSMO 2.0

A toast to New York's ever-evolving cocktail culture, this updated cosmo swaps out the old-school for fresh, vibrant ingredients. Cucumber-infused gin or vodka and yuzu juice bring crispness, while Aperol and cranberry syrup balance citrus with subtle sweetness. The finishing touch: a dash of orange flower water, imparting a subtle floral complexity to this refreshing cocktail. For a quick infusion, muddle fresh cucumber slices in the shaker before making the cocktail.

1½ ounces cucumber-infused vodka or gin (see Note)

¾ ounce yuzu juice

½ ounce Aperol

½ ounce Cranberry Simple Syrup (page 226)

2 drops orange blossom water

1 edible flower, for garnish

In a cocktail shaker filled with ice, combine the vodka, yuzu juice, Aperol, simple syrup, and orange blossom water. Cover and shake vigorously until well chilled, then strain into a chilled Nick and Nora or martini glass. Garnish with a flower and serve.

NOTE

To make cucumber-infused vodka, slice half of a cucumber into thin rounds and place them in a clean jar or bottle. Pour 1 cup of vodka over the cucumber slices, ensuring they are fully submerged. Seal the container and store it in the refrigerator for at least 1 day or up to 3 days, shaking it gently once a day. After the infusion period, strain out the cucumber slices and transfer the infused vodka to a clean bottle or jar.

MAKES 1 DRINK

Classic CHERRY BOUNCE

Cherry Bounce has deep historical roots in North Carolina, particularly in the Appalachian regions, where early settlers preserved summer's harvest by infusing local cherries in brandy or bourbon. Whether made with sweet or sour cherries, this homemade spirit became a Southern tradition, often enjoyed at gatherings or through the long winter months, and remains a beloved tribute to the state's agricultural heritage.

- 2 cups bourbon or brandy
- 1 cup sugar
- 2 cups pitted fresh cherries, sweet or sour (about 12 ounces)
- ¼ cinnamon stick
- 1 allspice berry

In a 2-quart glass jar with a lid, combine the bourbon or brandy and sugar. Cover and shake the mixture until the sugar dissolves. Add the cherries, cinnamon stick, and allspice berry. Seal the jar and shake gently to mix the ingredients. Store the jar in a cool, dark place for 6 weeks to 3 months, shaking it occasionally.

When it's ready to your liking, strain the mixture through a fine-mesh strainer into a bowl, discarding the cherries and spices. Let it sit overnight so any sediment sinks to the bottom of the bowl.

Carefully ladle the cherry bounce into a clean 1-quart jar with a lid. Store at room temperature or refrigerate for up to 1 year.

MAKES 1 DRINK

Modern TAR HEEL TWIST

The Tar Heel Twist blends North Carolina's rich traditions in farming and distilling. Craft bourbon highlights the state's spirits scene, while Carolina Gold rice syrup adds historic Lowcountry sweetness. Sparkling peach cider, rosemary, and grilled peaches showcase the vibrant orchards and gardens that thrive across North Carolina's diverse landscapes.

2 ounces North Carolina craft bourbon

¾ ounce Toasted Carolina Gold Rice Simple Syrup (page 224) or a mild rice syrup

1 ounce fresh lemon juice

½ ounce rosemary infusion (see Note)

2 ounces sparkling peach cider

1 grilled peach slice, for garnish

1 fresh rosemary sprig, for garnish

Fill a cocktail shaker with ice. Add the bourbon, simple syrup, lemon juice, and rosemary infusion. Cover and shake vigorously until chilled. Strain into an ice-filled collins or highball glass. Top with sparkling peach cider and gently stir. Garnish with the grilled peach slice and rosemary sprig.

NOTE

To make a rosemary infusion, steep 1 to 2 fresh rosemary sprigs in ¼ cup hot water for about 10 minutes. Strain and cool before using.

MAKES 1 DRINK

Classic NORTH DAKOTA SPECIAL

In North Dakota, rugged independence and a taste for strong spirits come together in this bold cocktail. Drawing on the state's love for whiskey—especially Canadian imports from across the northern border—this drink mixes bourbon, whiskey, peach liqueur, and Coca-Cola for a bracing, no-frills cheer to North Dakota's frontier spirit.

- 1 ounce Canadian whiskey, such as Crown Royal
- 1 ounce Jack Daniel's whiskey
- 1 ounce Wild Turkey bourbon
- ½ ounce peach liqueur
- 4 ounces Coca-Cola
- 1 peach slice or lemon wheel, for garnish (optional)

Fill a pint glass with ice. Add the Canadian whiskey, Jack Daniel's, Wild Turkey, and peach liqueur. Top with Coca-Cola and gently stir. Garnish with a peach slice or lemon wheel (if using) and serve.

MAKES 1 DRINK

Modern PRAIRIE ROSE

Named for North Dakota's state flower, the prairie rose, this cocktail celebrates the state's wild beauty and agricultural abundance. Rye whiskey—long favored on the Plains—meets a rich syrup of native chokecherries, honey, and hibiscus. A splash each of rose water and sparkling water lifts it into something earthy, floral, and unmistakably North Dakotan.

- 2 ounces rye whiskey, preferably from North Dakota
- 1 ounce Hibiscus-Chokecherry Honey Simple Syrup (page 224)
- 2 or 3 drops rose water
- 2 ounces sparkling water
- Dried sugared rose petals, for garnish

Fill a cocktail shaker with ice. Add the rye whiskey, simple syrup, and rose water. Shake briefly to chill, then strain into an ice-filled rocks glass. Top with sparkling water and gently stir. Garnish with dried sugared rose petals and serve.

MAKES 1 DRINK

Classic 1803

Named for the year Ohio gained statehood, this cocktail layers flavors tied to the state's geography and history. Tart cherry juice evokes northern orchards near Lake Erie, while sweet strawberries honor the state's summer harvests. A splash of balsamic vinegar recalls Ohio's robust food scene. Ohio's 1803 is bold, homegrown, and refreshingly complex—true to its Midwestern roots.

- 2 ripe strawberries, hulled, plus 1 small strawberry for garnish
- 2 ounces tart cherry juice
- 1½ ounces vodka
- ½ ounce dry vermouth
- ½ ounce Simple Syrup (page 223)
- ½ teaspoon balsamic vinegar
- 1 orange twist, for garnish

In a cocktail shaker, muddle 2 strawberries until crushed. Fill the shaker with ice and add the cherry juice, vodka, dry vermouth, simple syrup, and balsamic vinegar. Cover and shake vigorously until chilled. Strain into an ice-filled rocks glass. Garnish with the remaining strawberry and the orange twist and serve.

MAKES 1 DRINK

Modern OHIO ORCHARD FIZZ

This modern cocktail celebrates the Buckeye State's seasonal bounty and spirited legacy. Fresh-pressed apple juice reflects Ohio's top ranking in Midwest apple production—especially from the orchards of northeastern counties—and dark cherries celebrate the state's summer harvests. Bourbon honors the state's whiskey roots, tying the cocktail to Ohio's pre-Prohibition distilling history. Topped with ginger beer and a dash of bitters, it's a vibrant reflection on Ohio tradition.

---

3 pitted dark cherries, plus 1 whole cherry with stem, for garnish

4 fresh basil or mint leaves, plus 1 small sprig for garnish

1½ ounces bourbon or gin

1½ ounces fresh, unfiltered apple juice

½ ounce cherry liqueur, such as Heering

½ ounce fresh lemon juice

2 dashes Angostura bitters

3 ounces ginger beer

In a cocktail shaker, muddle the 3 pitted cherries and basil or mint leaves until well broken down. Fill the shaker with ice and add the bourbon or gin, apple juice, cherry liqueur, lemon juice, and bitters. Cover and shake vigorously until chilled. Strain into an ice-filled highball or collins glass. Top with ginger beer and stir gently to combine. Garnish with the cherry and herb sprig and serve.

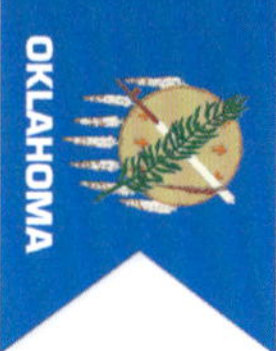

MAKES 1 DRINK

Classic LUNCHBOX

Created in the 1990s at Edna's, a beloved Oklahoma City dive bar, the Lunchbox blends light beer, orange juice, and a shot of amaretto. Its unexpected flavor and easy appeal made it a local legend. Still popular today, it's a signature of OKC's unpretentious, inventive bar culture.

- 5 ounces cold fresh orange juice
- 6 ounces ice-cold light beer, preferably Coors Light
- 1 ounce amaretto
- 1 orange slice, for garnish

Freeze a beer mug until frosty. Add the orange juice, then the beer and stir gently to mix. Pour in the amaretto, garnish with the orange slice, and serve.

MAKES 1 DRINK

Modern SOONER SIPPER

This cocktail highlights Oklahoma's agricultural heritage. Pecan-washed bourbon salutes to the state's top pecan production, while sorghum syrup and black walnut bitters evoke traditional crops and wild flavors. Porter peaches from northeastern Oklahoma add sweet richness, rounded out with a hint of mesquite smoke.

- Mesquite wood chip (for smoke)
- 2 ounces pecan-washed bourbon (see Note)
- 1 ounce fresh peach juice or peach puree, preferably from Porter peaches
- ½ ounce fresh lemon juice
- ½ ounce sorghum syrup or molasses
- 2 dashes black walnut or pecan bitters
- 1 peach slice, torched with a flame, for garnish

Place a mesquite wood chip on a heatproof surface. Using a match, light it on fire, blow it out, and invert a rocks glass over the smoldering wood chip to capture the smoke. Let it sit while you mix the cocktail.

In a cocktail shaker filled with ice, combine the pecan-washed bourbon, peach juice, lemon juice, sorghum syrup, and bitters. Cover and shake vigorously until chilled. Add a large ice cube to the smoky rocks glass, then strain the cocktail over the ice. Garnish with a torched peach slice.

NOTE

To make pecan-washed bourbon, combine 1 cup bourbon with ¼ cup toasted pecans. Let sit at room temperature for 24 hours, then freeze for 2 hours. Strain through cheesecloth to remove solids. Store in a sealed container.

MAKES 1 DRINK

Classic SPANISH COFFEE

Invented in the 1970s at Huber's Café—Portland's oldest restaurant—Spanish coffee is a regional classic. Their dramatic twist on a Spanish-style coffee cocktail combines flaming rum and triple sec with Kahlúa and hot coffee. Huber's signature cold-weather drink remains a staple of Oregon cocktail culture and a must-see spectacle in downtown Portland, showcasing Oregon's flair.

- 1 small lemon wedge
- 1 tablespoon sugar
- ¾ ounce 151-proof rum
- ½ ounce orange liqueur, preferably triple sec
- 1 pinch ground cinnamon
- 1 pinch freshly grated nutmeg
- 1 ounce coffee liqueur, preferably Kahlúa
- 4 ounces hot brewed coffee
- Lightly whipped cream, for topping

Rub the rim of a tempered fireproof glass (such as an Irish coffee glass) with the lemon wedge. Spread the sugar on a saucer and dip the rim of the glass in the sugar to coat the edges.

Add the rum and orange liqueur to the glass and carefully ignite the mixture using a long lighter. Sprinkle cinnamon and nutmeg into the flame to create aromatic sparks. Pour in the Kahlúa and hot coffee to extinguish the flame and mix the drink. Float whipped cream on top by gently pouring it over the back of a spoon. Serve immediately.

MAKES 1 DRINK

Modern
OREGON ROSE FIZZ

With its lush blackberries, delicate rose accents, and sparkling rosé, this contemporary cocktail captures the Pacific Northwest's bounty and flair. Reflecting Oregon's farm-to-glass ethos and Portland's vibrant cocktail culture, this drink celebrates the state's natural beauty and creative spirit in every elegant sip.

- 3 fresh blackberries
- 2 ounces vodka
- ¾ ounce Rose Petal Simple Syrup (page 223)
- ½ ounce fresh lemon juice
- 2 ounces cold sparkling rosé
- Fresh food-grade rose petals or skewered blackberries, for garnish

---

In a cocktail shaker, muddle the blackberries until broken down. Fill the shaker with ice and add the vodka, simple syrup, and lemon juice. Cover and shake vigorously until chilled. Strain into a chilled Nick and Nora or coupe glass. Top with sparking rose. Garnish with rose petals or a blackberry skewer and serve.

MAKES 1 DRINK

Classic CLOVER CLUB

Originally crafted in pre-Prohibition Philadelphia, the Clover Club cocktail blends gin, raspberry, lemon, and egg white into a bright, balanced drink. Though it began in an exclusive men's club, today it represents Pennsylvania's long-standing cocktail tradition—reimagined for a modern, inclusive bar culture that welcomes everyone to the table.

---

2 ounces gin

¾ ounce fresh lemon juice

½ ounce raspberry simple syrup (page 226) or grenadine

½ ounce egg white

Fresh raspberries speared with a cocktail pick, or 1 lemon twist, for garnish

---

Add the gin, lemon juice, simple syrup, and egg white to a cocktail shaker. Cover and shake vigorously for 30 seconds. Fill the shaker with ice, cover, and continue to shake until well chilled and frothy. Strain into a chilled coupe or Nick and Nora glass. Garnish with a few raspberries or a lemon twist and serve.

MAKES 1 DRINK

Modern
MIDNIGHT MYCELIUM

Pennsylvania's legacy as a rye whiskey stronghold anchors this cocktail, while its dense forests make it a forager's haven for wild mushrooms. Locally produced maple syrup and a thriving coffee-roasting scene inspire ingredients that round out the flavors. Midnight Mycelium brings together the state's agricultural richness and craft beverage culture in one bold pour.

1½ ounces mushroom-infused rye whiskey (see Note)

1 ounce cold brew coffee

¼ ounce maple syrup

2 dashes orange or black walnut bitters

1 orange twist, for garnish

In a cocktail shaker half filled with ice, combine the mushroom-infused rye, cold brew coffee, maple syrup, and bitters. Stir gently with a bar spoon until chilled. Add a large ice cube to a rocks glass, then strain the cocktail over the ice. Express an orange twist over the glass and drop it in as garnish.

NOTE

To make mushroom-infused rye whiskey, in a jar, combine 1 cup rye whiskey with 2 or 3 dried mushrooms, such as porcini or shiitake. Let sit at room temperature for 6 to 12 hours, or until infused to your liking. Strain through cheesecloth to remove solids. Store in a sealed container.

MAKES 1 DRINK

Classic RHODE ISLAND RED

Created in 2005 to celebrate the 350th anniversary of Rhode Island's Royal Charter, the Rhode Island red cocktail honors the state's rich history, vibrant spirit, and growing craft-cocktail scene. Highlighting "pick-your-own" raspberry farms, this drink combines tequila, raspberry liqueur, and ginger beer for a refreshing local tribute.

- 5 fresh raspberries
- 2 ounces tequila
- ¾ ounce raspberry liqueur, such as Chambord
- ½ ounce fresh lemon juice
- 2 dashes orange bitters
- 3 ounces ginger beer
- 1 lemon twist, for garnish

In a cocktail shaker, muddle 4 of the raspberries until they're broken down. Fill the shaker with ice and add the tequila, raspberry liqueur, lemon juice, and orange bitters. Cover and shake vigorously until chilled. Strain into a chilled ice-filled highball or collins glass. Top with ginger beer and gently stir with a bar spoon. Garnish with the remaining raspberry and the lemon twist and serve.

MAKES 1 DRINK

Modern BRINY BREEZE

The Briny Breeze uses Narragansett lager, Rhode Island's beloved local beer, as a base. Clam juice nods to the state's shellfish industry, while tomato juice and yuzu add a contemporary twist on the michelada. For a simplified version, use Clamato in place of tomato water and clam juice.

- 1 small lemon wedge
- 1 teaspoon nori salt or seaweed salt (see Note), for rimming the glass
- 1 ounce fresh tomato juice
- ½ ounce clam juice (optional)
- ½ ounce yuzu juice or Meyer lemon juice
- 2 dashes celery bitters
- 1 pinch smoked paprika
- 6 ounces American-style lager, preferably Narragansett lager
- 1 lemon wheel, edges charred with a lighter or match, for garnish

---

Rim a highball or collins glass with the lemon wedge, dip the rim in nori salt, and fill the glass halfway with ice. In a cocktail shaker filled with ice, combine the tomato juice, clam juice, yuzu, bitters, and paprika, then strain into the glass.

Top with the lager, stir gently, and garnish with the charred lemon wheel.

NOTE

To make nori salt, tear 1 sheet of dried nori seaweed into small pieces. In a small food processor or spice grinder, pulse the nori and ¼ cup flaky sea salt together until the nori is finely ground and mixed with the salt. Store in an airtight container for up to 1 month.

MAKES 1 DRINK

Classic LOWCOUNTRY SPIKED SWEET TEA

Sweet tea is a staple of South Carolina life, from porches to picnics. This regional favorite blends locally distilled bourbon or vodka with lemon and honey for balance, while optional peach bitters nod to the state's fruit-growing heritage. It's a simple, familiar drink elevated with a touch of Lowcountry nuance.

---

2 ounces South Carolina bourbon or vodka

4 ounces strong brewed black tea, chilled

1 ounce Honey Simple Syrup (page 224)

½ ounce lemon juice

2 dashes peach bitters

1 lemon wheel, for garnish

1 fresh mint sprig, for garnish

In a cocktail shaker filled with ice, combine the bourbon, brewed tea, simple syrup, lemon juice, and peach bitters. Cover and shake vigorously until chilled. Strain into a tall, ice-filled glass, such as a pint glass. Garnish with the lemon wheel and mint sprig and serve.

MAKES 1 DRINK

Modern CAROLINA GOLD PUNCH

This updated version of the classic planter's punch celebrates South Carolina's coastal heritage, blending rum, pineapple, and a spiced cinnamon syrup made with toasted Carolina Gold rice. While acknowledging the region's complex colonial history and legacy of trade, it also reflects the South's enduring love of punch and the Lowcountry's rich traditions.

1½ ounces dark rum

½ ounce brandy

¾ ounce fresh lime juice

1 ounce pineapple juice

¾ ounce Carolina Gold Rice Cinnamon Simple Syrup (page 224) or Simple Syrup (page 223)

¼ ounce grenadine

2 dashes Angostura or peach bitters

1 ounce club soda

1 small mint sprig, for garnish

1 lime wheel, for garnish

In a cocktail shaker filled with ice, combine the rum, brandy, lime juice, pineapple juice, simple syrup, grenadine, and bitters. Cover and shake vigorously until chilled. Strain into an ice-filled highball glass. Top with the club soda and stir gently with a bar spoon. Garnish with the mint sprig and lime wheel and serve.

MAKES 1 DRINK

Classic
SOUTH DAKOTA MARTINI

The South Dakota martini riffs on red beer (page 120) traditions with light lager, tomato juice, and pickle brine, plus a pickle spear garnish—flavors rooted in Midwestern bar culture and farmhouse pantries. In a state known for its love of pickles and practical fare, variations with olive juice and speared olives offer a salty twist on this prairie classic.

- 3 ounces tomato juice, chilled
- 1 ounce dill pickle juice
- 8 ounces light beer, preferably on draft
- 1 dill pickle spear, for garnish

Pour the tomato juice and pickle juice into a pint glass. Top with beer and stir gently. Garnish with the pickle spear and serve.

MAKES 1 DRINK

Modern
SAGE PLAINS BREEZE

A mix of bourbon, wild plum shrub, and honey syrup with a pinch of salt captures the spirit of South Dakota in this contemporary cocktail that balances bold flavors and simplicity. Fresh sage and lemon add earthy and bright notes, reflecting the state's untamed plains and natural beauty.

- 4 fresh sage leaves
- 1½ ounces bourbon
- 1 ounce Wild Plum Shrub (page 227)
- ½ ounce Honey Simple Syrup (page 224)
- 1 pinch kosher salt
- ¾ ounce fresh lemon juice
- ½ ounce egg white
- 1 fresh sage sprig and/or 1 lemon twist, for garnish

In a cocktail shaker, muddle the fresh sage leaves to release their oils. Add the bourbon, wild plum shrub, simple syrup, salt, lemon juice, and egg white. Cover and shake vigorously for 30 seconds. Fill the shaker with ice, cover, and continue to shake until well chilled and frothy. Strain into a coupe glass. Garnish with the sage sprig and/or lemon twist and serve.

MAKES 1 DRINK

Classic LYNCHBURG LEMONADE

The Lynchburg lemonade was created in the 1980s at Miss Mary Bobo's Restaurant in Lynchburg, Tennessee, near the Jack Daniel's distillery. This refreshing cocktail blends the bold flavor of Jack Daniel's whiskey with citrus and soda, celebrating Tennessee's rich distilling legacy and Southern hospitality. For a less sweet version, use club soda.

- 1½ ounces Jack Daniel's whiskey
- 1 ounce triple sec
- 1 ounce fresh lemon juice
- 4 ounces lemon-lime soda
- 1 lemon wheel, for garnish
- 1 mint sprig, for garnish

In a cocktail shaker filled with ice, combine the whiskey, triple sec, and lemon juice. Cover and shake vigorously until chilled. Strain into an ice-filled highball glass. Top with the lemon-lime soda and stir gently with a bar spoon. Garnish with the lemon wheel and mint sprig and serve.

MAKES 1 DRINK

Modern HARVEST

This modern Southern cocktail celebrates Tennessee's fall flavors, blending local Tennessee whiskey with cold-pressed apple cider and pecan syrup, reflecting the state's connection to its natural bounty. Frangelico adds a nutty depth, while fresh lemon juice and bitters balance the sweetness, capturing the essence of the season in a vibrant, warming drink.

- 2 ounces Tennessee whiskey
- 1 ounce cold-pressed apple cider
- ½ ounce Toasted Pecan Simple Syrup (page 223)
- ½ ounce Frangelico
- ½ ounce fresh lemon juice
- 2 dashes Angostura bitters
- 1 thin apple slice, for garnish

In a cocktail shaker filled with ice, combine the whiskey, apple cider, simple syrup, Frangelico, lemon juice, and bitters. Cover and shake vigorously until chilled. Strain into an ice-filled rocks glass. Garnish with the apple slice and serve.

MAKES 1 DRINK

Classic MARGARITA

Although the classic margarita originated in Mexico, it has become a beloved fixture in Texas bars, restaurants, and cantinas, highlighting the state's strong connection to Mexican heritage and its vibrant border culture. The frozen margarita, a Texas innovation, was first created in Dallas in the 1970s, further cementing its place in the state's drink history.

- Kosher salt, for rimming the glass
- 1 lime wedge
- 2 ounces blanco tequila
- 1½ ounces triple sec
- 1 ounce fresh lime juice
- 1 lime slice, for garnish

Pour the salt onto a small plate. Gently rub the lime wedge around the rim of a rocks or coupe glass. Holding the base of the glass, dip the rim into the salt. Fill the glass half full of ice, if you like.

Fill a cocktail shaker with ice. Add the tequila, triple sec, and lime juice. Cover, shake vigorously, and strain into the glass. Garnish with the lime slice.

MAKES 1 DRINK

Modern CILANTRO CITRUS RANCH WATER

Cilantro Citrus Ranch Water modernizes Texas's classic ranch water, a cocktail originally created by West Texas ranchers as a simple, refreshing mix of tequila, lime, and Topo Chico sparkling water. This updated version infuses muddled cilantro, jalapeño, and orange with a splash of grapefruit juice and a pinch of chile salt, capturing the bold, sunny spirit and vibrant flavors of Texas.

---

3 fresh cilantro sprigs

2 slices fresh jalapeño

1 fresh orange slice

2 ounces blanco tequila

1 ounce fresh lime juice

1 ounce fresh grapefruit juice

1 pinch chile salt, chile-lime seasoning, or smoked salt

3 ounces sparkling water, preferably Topo Chico

1 thin orange or grapefruit wheel, for garnish

In a cocktail shaker, muddle 2 of the cilantro sprigs with the jalapeño and the orange slice. Fill the shaker with ice and add the tequila, lime juice, grapefruit juice, and chile salt. Cover and shake until well chilled. Strain into an ice-filled pint glass. Top with the Topo Chico and stir gently. Garnish with the remaining cilantro sprig and the citrus wheel and serve.

UTAH

MAKES 1 DRINK

Classic
DIRTY SODA

Originating as a popular Utah mocktail, the dirty soda blends Diet Coke, heavy cream, coconut syrup, and lime for a creamy, tangy twist on the classic cola. Although dirty soda was originally non-alcoholic and favored in Mormon culture, this version optionally adds rum, transforming the nostalgic favorite into a quirky, indulgent cocktail.

- 1 ounce dark rum (optional)
- ½ ounce coconut syrup
- ½ ounce fresh lime juice
- 5 ounces diet or regular soda, preferably Diet Coke
- ½ ounce heavy whipping cream
- 1 lime wedge, for garnish

In a chilled rocks glass, stir together the rum (if using), coconut syrup, and lime juice. Fill the glass with ice, then top with the soda. Stir gently with a bar spoon. Top with the cream, garnish with a lime wedge, and serve.

MAKES 1 DRINK

Modern JUNIPER RIDGE

Inspired by Utah's rugged alpine landscapes and local flora, this modern cocktail captures the state's essence in a glass. Featuring juniper berries reminiscent of high desert terrain, native pine nuts, and tart cherries—Utah's state fruit—this gin-based drink balances earthy botanicals with bright citrus and a sparkling finish.

Leaves of 1 small rosemary sprig, plus 1 whole small sprig for garnish

2 juniper berries

2 ounces gin

¾ ounce tart cherry simple syrup (page 226)

½ ounce pine nut–infused dry vermouth (see Note)

½ ounce fresh lemon juice

2 ounces club soda

In a cocktail shaker, lightly muddle the rosemary leaves and juniper berries. Fill the shaker with ice and add the gin, simple syrup, vermouth, and lemon juice. Cover and shake until well chilled. Strain into an ice-filled highball glass. Top with the club soda and stir gently. Garnish with the rosemary sprig and serve.

NOTE

To make pine nut–infused vermouth, combine ½ cup dry vermouth with 2 tablespoons lightly toasted pine nuts in a jar. Let sit at room temperature for 24 to 48 hours, then strain. Store in the refrigerator and use within 2 weeks.

VERMONT

MAKES 1 DRINK

Classic
OLD VERMONT GIMLET

This cocktail honors Vermont's rich maple-syrup heritage, a key part of the state's identity since Indigenous peoples first tapped sugar maples centuries ago. A bright twist on the classic gimlet, it blends gin, citrus, bitters, and real maple syrup, balancing acidity with sweetness to celebrate Vermont's tradition of artisanal craft and flavor.

2½ ounces gin

1 ounce orange juice

½ ounce lemon juice

½ ounce maple syrup

2 dashes Angostura or orange bitters

1 orange twist, for garnish

Fill a cocktail shaker with ice. Add the gin, orange juice, lemon juice, maple syrup, and bitters. Cover and shake vigorously until chilled. Strain into a chilled coupe glass. Garnish with the orange twist and serve.

MAKES 1 DRINK

Modern WHITE MAPLE

The White Maple cocktail draws inspiration from Vermont's abundant white maples, known for their distinct pale bark. Blending bourbon, Vermont maple cream liqueur, cold brew coffee, and bitters, this drink captures the state's rich maple syrup heritage, finishing with a refreshing citrus and herbal garnish, reflecting Vermont's handcrafted flavors.

- 1½ ounces bourbon
- 1 ounce Vermont maple cream liqueur (see Note)
- 1 ounce cold brew coffee
- 2 dashes orange bitters
- 2 dashes coffee bitters
- 1 orange twist, for garnish
- 1 small rosemary sprig, for garnish

Fill a cocktail shaker with ice. Add the bourbon, maple cream liqueur, coffee, orange bitters, and coffee bitters. Cover and shake vigorously until chilled. Strain into an old-fashioned glass over a large ice cube. Garnish with the orange twist and rosemary sprig and serve.

NOTE

If you can't find maple cream liqueur, make your own with ½ ounce cognac, ¼ ounce maple syrup, and ¼ ounce heavy cream.

MAKES 1 DRINK

Classic
VIRGINIA WHISKEY SOUR

The whiskey sour, a classic cocktail of rye whiskey, lemon juice, and sugar, has deep roots in Virginia, where whiskey production dates back to the eighteenth century. By using one of America's earliest distilled spirits, the drink reflects Virginia's history as a key player in the nation's bourbon and rye traditions.

---

2 ounces rye whiskey or bourbon

¾ ounce fresh lemon juice

½ ounce Honey Simple Syrup (page 224)

1 orange slice, for garnish

1 maraschino cherry, for garnish

Fill a cocktail shaker with ice. Add the whiskey, lemon juice, and simple syrup. Cover and shake vigorously until chilled. Strain into a chilled rocks or coupe glass. Garnish with the orange slice and maraschino cherry and serve.

MAKES 1 DRINK

Modern

THE HUNTSMAN

This contemporary cocktail captures the adventurous spirit of Virginia's wilderness, where hunting and outdoor pursuits are deeply embedded in the culture. Inspired by the state's rugged landscapes, The Huntsman combines bourbon, grapefruit juice, honey syrup, and tarragon, all enhanced by a tangy citrus salt rim—reflecting Virginia's wild terrain and its long-standing tradition of crafting bold, flavorful spirits.

---

1 teaspoon kosher salt, for rimming the glass

¼ teaspoon finely grated grapefruit zest, for rimming the glass

1 small grapefruit wedge

4 fresh tarragon leaves

1½ ounces bourbon

1 ounce fresh grapefruit juice

½ ounce Honey Simple Syrup (page 224)

1 small tarragon sprig, for garnish

Combine the salt and grapefruit zest on a saucer and rub them together. Gently rub the grapefruit wedge around the rim of a coupe glass. Holding the base of the glass, dip the rim into the citrus salt.

In a cocktail shaker, lightly muddle the tarragon leaves. Fill the shaker with ice and add the bourbon, grapefruit juice, and simple syrup. Cover and shake until well chilled. Strain into the prepared glass. Garnish with the tarragon sprig and serve.

WASHINGTON

MAKES 1 DRINK

Classic APPLE MARTINI

The apple martini brings the crisp essence of Washington's famous apples to life. With more than 175 varieties grown across the state, Washington is the top apple producer in the United States. This cocktail blends vodka, apple schnapps, and cranberry juice, celebrating the state's bountiful harvest and fresh, vibrant flavors.

- 2 ounces vodka or gin
- ¾ ounce apple schnapps
- 1 ounce cranberry juice
- 1 thin apple slice, for garnish

Fill a cocktail shaker with ice. Add the vodka, apple schnapps, and cranberry juice. Cover and shake vigorously until chilled. Strain into a chilled martini or coupe glass. Garnish with the apple slice and serve.

MAKES 1 DRINK

Modern HOPPED-UP CHERRY

Washington leads the nation in sweet cherry and hops production, making it the perfect birthplace for this refreshing, beer-forward cocktail. The Hopped-Up Cherry blends lush local cherries, aromatic basil, botanical gin, and hoppy IPA—celebrating the state's agricultural abundance and deep-rooted love of bold, craft-driven flavor, especially in its beer culture.

- 4 fresh sweet Rainier cherries or dark sweet cherries, pitted
- 4 fresh basil leaves
- 1½ ounces botanical gin, preferably herbal or floral gin
- ¾ ounce sweet cherry simple syrup (page 226)
- ½ ounce lime juice
- 3 ounces hoppy beer, such as IPA
- 1 fresh sweet Rainier or dark sweet cherry with stem, for garnish
- 1 small sprig fresh basil, for garnish

In a cocktail shaker, muddle the pitted cherries and basil leaves. Fill the shaker with ice and add the gin, simple syrup, and lime juice. Cover and shake until well chilled. Strain into an ice-filled pint glass. Top with the beer and stir gently. Garnish with the cherry and basil sprig and serve.

MAKES 1 DRINK

Classic GIN RICKEY

The gin Rickey is Washington, DC's official native cocktail, born in the late nineteenth century at Shoomaker's bar. It was named after Democratic lobbyist Colonel Joe Rickey, who preferred his whiskey with soda and lime—though gin soon became the norm. Refreshing and low in sugar, it's a classic capital-city cooler.

- 2 ounces gin
- ½ ounce fresh lime juice
- 4 ounces club soda
- 1 lime wedge or wheel, for garnish

Fill a highball glass with ice. Add the gin and lime juice. Top with club soda and stir gently. Garnish with the lime wedge and serve.

MAKES 1 DRINK

Modern

MODERN SALTY DOG

A modern twist on the mid-century salty dog—originally a simple vodka or gin and grapefruit cocktail with a salted rim—this version nods to Washington, DC's naval history and political slang. The name evokes both navy traditions and sharp-tongued capitol characters, while kombucha and salted honey bring the drink into the present day.

- 1 teaspoon kosher salt, for rimming the glass
- ¼ teaspoon finely grated grapefruit zest, for rimming the glass
- 1 small grapefruit wedge
- 2 small sprigs rosemary
- 1½ ounces vodka
- 1 ounce fresh grapefruit juice
- 1 ounce grapefruit or citrus kombucha
- ¼ ounce fresh lime juice
- ¼ ounce Honey Simple Syrup (page 224)
- 1 pinch kosher salt
- 2 dashes grapefruit bitters
- 1 grapefruit peel twist, for garnish

Combine the salt and grapefruit zest on a saucer and rub them together. Gently rub the grapefruit wedge around the rim of a chilled coupe glass. Holding the base of the glass, dip the rim into the salt.

In a cocktail shaker, lightly muddle 1 of the rosemary sprigs. Fill the cocktail shaker with ice. Add the vodka, grapefruit juice, kombucha, lime juice, simple syrup, salt, and bitters. Cover and shake vigorously until chilled. Strain into the prepared glass.

Twist and squeeze the grapefruit peel over the drink, then drop the twist into the cocktail. Garnish with the remaining rosemary sprig and serve.

MAKES 1 DRINK

Classic APPALACHIAN DAIQUIRI

This bright, local twist on a classic daiquiri celebrates the pawpaw—North America's largest native fruit and a hidden gem of West Virginia's forests. Long foraged in the Appalachian region, the custard-like fruit has tropical notes of banana and mango. Use pawpaw puree, or try muddling a fresh deseeded pawpaw in the cocktail shaker. If you can't get pawpaw, sub in mango puree to evoke its flavor.

- 2 ounces white rum
- 1 ounce pawpaw puree or mango puree
- ¾ ounce lime juice
- ½ ounce Simple Syrup (page 223)
- 1 thin lime wheel, for garnish

Fill a cocktail shaker with ice. Add the rum, pawpaw puree, lime juice, and simple syrup. Cover and shake vigorously until chilled. Strain into a chilled coupe glass. Garnish with the lime wheel and serve.

MAKES 1 DRINK

Modern
GREAT LAUREL MARTINI

In West Virginia, the rhododendron—also known as the great laurel—blooms abundantly across the state's rugged terrain. This cocktail draws inspiration from the region's wild beauty, featuring foraged blackberries and elderflower liqueur, elements reflective of the state's rich flora. Lavender bitters add an aromatic touch, embodying West Virginia's untamed spirit.

- 1½ ounces botanical gin
- ½ ounce blackberry simple syrup (page 226)
- ½ ounce elderflower liqueur
- ½ ounce fresh lemon juice
- 2 dashes lavender bitters
- 1 small fresh lavender sprig, for garnish

Fill a cocktail shaker with ice. Add the gin, simple syrup, elderflower liqueur, lemon juice, and lavender bitters. Cover and shake vigorously until chilled. Strain into a chilled martini or coupe glass. Garnish with the lavender sprig and serve.

MAKES 1 DRINK

Classic BRANDY OLD-FASHIONED

The brandy old-fashioned is Wisconsin's unofficial state cocktail, a beloved twist on the classic. Popularized after World War II by returning soldiers and fueled by the state's preference for brandy over whiskey, it's traditionally muddled with cherries and orange, then topped with soda—sweet, approachable, and distinctly Wisconsinite in style.

- 3 dashes Angostura bitters
- 1 thin orange wedge
- 1 thin lemon wedge
- 2 maraschino cherries
- 1 sugar cube
- 2½ ounces brandy

In an old-fashioned glass, combine the bitters, orange wedge, lemon wedge, cherries, and sugar cube. Muddle the ingredients in the bottom of the glass. Fill the glass with ice, add the brandy, stir well, and serve.

MAKES 1 DRINK

Modern NORTHWOODS BUTTER RUM

This cozy cocktail is a tribute to Wisconsin's Northwoods—where pine forests, frozen lakes, and cabin life define the landscape. Butter-washed rum pays homage to the state's dairy roots, while cranberries—one of Wisconsin's top crops—bring tart warmth. A hint of smoke and citrus evokes woodstoves, snowy trails, and long winter nights up north.

- 2 ounces butter-washed dark rum (see Note)
- ¾ ounce Spiced Cranberry Simple Syrup (page 226)
- 2 dashes Angostura bitters
- 1 pinch smoked sea salt
- 1 orange peel, made with a vegetable peeler

Fill a cocktail shaker with ice. Add the rum, simple syrup, bitters, and salt. Cover and shake vigorously until chilled. Strain into a chilled rocks glass over a large ice cube. Light a match, then twist and squeeze the orange peel over the flame. Rub the peel around the rim of the glass, drop it into the drink, and serve.

NOTE

To make butter-washed rum, melt 2 tablespoons unsalted butter and combine with ½ cup dark rum in a jar. Let sit at room temperature for 1 hour, then refrigerate overnight. Once it has solidified, remove and discard the butter cap and strain the rum through a cheesecloth or coffee filter. Store in the fridge and use within 1 to 2 weeks.

WYOMING

MAKES 1 DRINK

Classic WYOMING RATTLESNAKE

Named for the rattlesnake and the rugged terrain it roams, this bold cocktail channels Wyoming's frontier spirit. Rye whiskey provides a spicy backbone, balanced by citrus and silky egg white, while a whisper of absinthe alludes to the state's wild edge. It's classic Western grit with a refined bite.

- 2 ounces rye whiskey
- ¾ ounce fresh lemon juice
- ½ ounce Simple Syrup (page 223)
- ¼ ounce absinthe
- ½ ounce egg white
- 1 lemon twist, for garnish

Add the rye whiskey, lemon juice, simple syrup, absinthe, and egg white to a cocktail shaker. Cover and shake vigorously for 30 seconds. Fill the shaker with ice, cover, and continue to shake until well chilled and frothy. Strain into a chilled coupe glass. Garnish with the lemon twist and serve.

MAKES 1 DRINK

Modern HIGH COUNTRY NEGRONI

This alpine Negroni channels the high-altitude essence of Wyoming, where juniper grows wild and huckleberries thrive in mountain meadows. Featuring locally made sweet vermouth and a hint of smoked aspen salt—a nod to the state's aspen groves and campfire culture—it's a rugged, aromatic cocktail rooted in the Wild West.

1 ounce botanical gin

1 ounce sweet vermouth, preferably from Wyoming

1 ounce dry vermouth, infused with juniper berries (see Note)

½ ounce Campari

½ ounce orange liqueur, such as Grand Marnier

½ ounce huckleberry simple syrup (page 226)

1 pinch smoked salt

1 juniper sprig, for garnish

Fill a cocktail shaker with ice. Add the gin, sweet vermouth, dry vermouth, Campari, orange liqueur, simple syrup, and smoked salt and shake to combine. Strain into an ice-filled rocks glass or a chilled coupe glass without ice. Garnish with the juniper sprig and serve.

NOTE

To make juniper berry–infused vermouth, combine ½ cup dry vermouth with 2 teaspoons juniper berries in a jar. Let sit at room temperature for 24 to 48 hours, then strain. Store in the refrigerator and use within 2 weeks.

SPIRITS GUIDE

BITTERS

Bitters—Highly concentrated flavoring agents made from herbs, roots, and spices, used in drops or dashes

BRANDY AND COGNAC

Apple brandy/Applejack—Brandy distilled from apples, ranging from light and fruity to robust

Apricot brandy—Sweet fruit brandy or liqueur flavored with apricots

Cognac—French grape brandy from the Cognac region, aged in oak for depth and elegance

FORTIFIED WINES AND APERITIFS

Apple vermouth—Vermouth infused with apple flavors for a fruity twist

Dry vermouth—Fortified wine flavored with herbs, a key martini ingredient

Ruby port—Sweet, fortified Portuguese wine with rich berry and spice flavors

GIN

Botanical gin—Modern style featuring unique botanicals like cucumber, lavender, or spices

London Dry gin—Classic gin style with strong juniper and citrus notes

LIQUEURS AND CORDIALS

Absinthe—Strong anise-flavored spirit traditionally associated with herbal complexity

Almond liqueur—General category for nut-based liqueurs, often used in desserts or cocktails

Amer Picon/Torani Amer/Ferino Amer—Bitter-orange French-style aperitifs used in classic cocktails

Amaretto—Sweet almond-flavored liqueur (e.g., Disaronno)

Aperol—Bright-orange Italian aperitivo with bitter orange and rhubarb notes

Black currant liqueur/crème de cassis—Deeply flavored liqueur made from black currants

Campari—Iconic Italian bitter with intense herbal and citrus flavors

Coffee liqueur—Sweet coffee-flavored liqueur (e.g., Kahlúa)

Crème de cacao—Chocolate-flavored liqueur, available in white or dark versions

Dark cherry liqueur—Rich, fruity liqueur (e.g., Heering cherry liqueur)

Elderflower liqueur—Floral liqueur with delicate, sweet flavors (e.g., St-Germain)

Irish cream—Creamy liqueur made with Irish whiskey and chocolate (e.g., Baileys)

Orange liqueur—Includes triple sec, curaçao, Cointreau, and Grand Marnier, all with citrus sweetness

Sloe gin—Liqueur made by infusing gin with sloe berries, tart and fruity

RUM

Dark rum—Aged rum with rich molasses, caramel, and spice notes

Overproof rum (151-proof rum)—Extra-strong rum used sparingly for bold cocktails or floats

White rum—Clear rum with a light, clean flavor, often used in refreshing cocktails

SYRUPS AND SWEETENERS

Grenadine—Nonalcoholic syrup made from pomegranate, used for sweetness and color

Orgeat—Sweet almond syrup (or variants like sunflower seed orgeat) with floral and nutty notes

TEQUILA & MEZCAL

Blanco tequila—Unaged tequila with crisp agave flavor and peppery finish

Mezcal—Smoky Mexican spirit distilled from agave, often with earthy and savory notes

VODKA

Orange vodka—Flavored vodka infused with orange for citrus-driven drinks

Vodka—Neutral spirit prized for smoothness and versatility in cocktails

WHISKEY

Bourbon—American whiskey made mostly from corn, known for caramel and vanilla notes

Canadian whiskey—Smooth, blended whiskey, often lighter in style

Corn whiskey—Light, sweet whiskey made almost entirely from corn

Rye—Spicy, bold whiskey with peppery and herbal flavors

Tennessee whiskey—Similar to bourbon but charcoal-filtered for mellowness (e.g., Jack Daniel's)

Whiskey (general)—Grain-based spirit distilled and aged in oak, varying by region and style

SYRUPS, SHRUBS, AND MORE

Simple Syrup

MAKES ABOUT ¾ CUP

½ cup water

½ cup sugar

Infuser of choice (optional; see list of infused syrups)

In a small saucepan over medium-high heat, bring the water to a simmer. Add the sugar and infuser of choice, if using, and stir until the sugar is dissolved.

Remove from the heat and let cool completely. For a stronger infusion, let sit for several hours or up to overnight. Strain the syrup through a fine-mesh sieve into a clean container, cover, and refrigerate for up to 2 weeks.

INFUSED SYRUPS

Ginger Simple Syrup:
1 tablespoon peeled and grated fresh ginger

Cinnamon-Ginger Simple Syrup:
1 tablespoon peeled and grated fresh ginger plus 1 cinnamon stick

5-Spice Simple Syrup:
1 teaspoon 5-spice powder

Lemon Balm Simple Syrup:
1 tablespoon chopped fresh lemon balm

Chamomile Simple Syrup:
1 tablespoon dried chamomile flowers

Spruce Tip Simple Syrup:
2 tablespoons chopped fresh spruce or fir tips

Rose Petal Simple Syrup:
1 tablespoon food-grade rose petals and ½ teaspoon rosewater

Basil-Mint Simple Syrup:
1 tablespoon chopped fresh basil and 2 teaspoons chopped fresh mint leaves

Sweet Tea–Basil Simple Syrup:
1 tablespoon chopped fresh basil plus 2 black tea bags

Toasted Pecan Simple Syrup:
2 tablespoons chopped toasted pecans

Sunflower Seed Orgeat

MAKES ABOUT 1 CUP

¼ cup water

¼ cup sugar

3 tablespoons unsalted sunflower seeds

In a small saucepan over medium-high heat, bring the water to a simmer. Add the sugar and sunflower seeds and stir until the sugar is dissolved and the mixture is steaming.

Remove from the heat and let cool completely. Set aside to steep for 12 to 24 hours at room temperature. Strain the syrup through a fine-mesh sieve into a clean container, cover, and refrigerate for up to 1 week.

Spiced Molasses Simple Syrup

MAKES ABOUT ¾ CUP

½ cup water

½ cup molasses

2 cinnamon sticks

4 whole star anise

½ teaspoon whole black peppercorns

In a small saucepan over medium-low heat, combine the water, molasses, cinnamon sticks, star anise, and peppercorns. Simmer, stirring occasionally, for 5 minutes. Strain the syrup through a fine-mesh sieve into a clean container, cover, and refrigerate for up to 2 weeks.

Honey Simple Syrup

MAKES 1 CUP

½ cup honey

½ cup water

Infuser of choice (optional; see list of infused syrups)

In a saucepan over medium-high heat, combine the honey, water, and infuser of your choice (if using), stirring until the honey melts into the water and the mixture is steaming. Remove from the heat and let cool completely.

Pour into a clean container (through a fine-mesh sieve if using an infuser), cover, and refrigerate for up to 2 weeks.

INFUSED HONEY SYRUPS

Lavender-Chile Honey Simple Syrup:
1 teaspoon chopped culinary lavender and 1 tablespoon seeded and chopped dried chile

Honey-Sage Simple Syrup:
3 fresh sage leaves

Hibiscus-Chokecherry Honey Simple Syrup:
½ cup chokecherries or pitted dark cherries and 2 tablespoons hibiscus tea

Toasted Carolina Gold Rice Simple Syrup

MAKES ABOUT ½ CUP

¼ cup water

¼ cup sugar

3 tablespoons unsalted sunflower seeds

In a small, dry sauté pan over medium heat, toast the rice until lightly browned and fragrant, about 4 minutes. Remove from the heat and pour the rice into a heatproof bowl. Carefully pour the simple syrup over the rice and stir to combine. Let cool completely. Strain the mixture through a fine-mesh sieve into a jar, discarding the rice.

VARIATION

Carolina Gold Rice Cinnamon Simple Syrup:
Add 1 cinnamon stick to the rice just before removing it from the heat; after straining, add the cinnamon stick to the simple syrup before storing.

Fruit Simple Syrups

MAKES ABOUT 1 CUP

¼ cup chopped fruit, such as raspberries, blackberries, huckleberries, (wild) blueberries, or pitted tart or sweet cherries

½ cup sugar

½ cup water

2 teaspoons fresh lemon juice

In a saucepan over medium-high heat, combine the fruit, sugar, water, and lemon juice and bring to a simmer. Reduce the heat to medium-low and continue to simmer, stirring frequently, smashing the fruit as you stir, until it has broken down and become juicy, about 5 minutes. Strain the syrup through a fine-mesh sieve into a clean container, cover, and refrigerate for up to 5 days.

VARIATIONS

Blackberry-Thyme Simple Syrup: Use blackberries and add 2 thyme sprigs to the mixture before simmering.

Blackberry-Mint Simple Syrup: Use blackberries and add 1 tablespoon chopped fresh mint leaves to the mixture before simmering.

Cranberry Simple Syrup

MAKES ABOUT ¾ CUP

½ cup pure unsweetened cranberry juice

½ cup sugar

In a small saucepan over medium-low heat, combine the cranberry juice and sugar. Stir until the sugar is dissolved, then remove from the heat and set aside to cool. Transfer to a clean container and refrigerate for up to 1 week.

VARIATION

Spiced Cranberry Simple Syrup: Add 1 cinnamon stick to the mixture before simmering, then stir in ½ teaspoon vanilla extract or vanilla paste once the syrup has cooled.

Lime Simple Syrup

MAKES ABOUT ¾ CUP

½ cup fresh lime juice

1 teaspoon finely grated lime zest

½ cup sugar

In a small saucepan over medium-low heat, combine the lime juice, zest, and sugar. Stir until the sugar is dissolved, then remove from the heat and set aside to cool. Strain through a fine-mesh sieve into a clean container and refrigerate for up to 1 week.

VARIATION

Lemon-Lime Simple Syrup: Usc ¼ cup lime juice and ¼ cup lemon juice plus ½ teaspoon zest of each.

Cranberry Shrub

MAKES ABOUT 1½ CUPS

1 cup pure cranberry juice

½ cup sugar

¼ cup apple cider vinegar

In a saucepan, combine the cranberry juice and sugar. Heat over medium heat until the sugar dissolves and the mixture is steaming. Remove from the heat and allow the mixture to cool to room temperature. Add the vinegar and stir well. Seal the jar and refrigerate for at least 24 hours, allowing the flavors to meld. Shake the jar occasionally. Use within 2 weeks.

Wild Plum Shrub

MAKES ABOUT 1½ CUPS

1 cup pitted and chopped fresh ripe wild (or purchased) plums

½ cup sugar

½ cup water

¼ cup apple cider vinegar

In a saucepan, combine the chopped plums, sugar, and water. Heat over medium heat, stirring occasionally, until the sugar dissolves and the plums begin to break down, about 5 minutes. Remove from the heat and allow to cool to room temperature. Once the mixture has cooled, mash the plums to release their juices.

Strain the mixture through a fine-mesh sieve or cheesecloth into a clean jar or bottle, pressing the solids to extract as much juice as possible.

Add the apple cider vinegar and stir to combine. Seal the jar and refrigerate for 3 to 5 days, allowing the flavors to meld. Shake the jar occasionally. Use within 2 weeks.

Cinnamon-Apple Simple Syrup

MAKES ABOUT ¾ CUP

½ cup unfiltered apple juice or apple cider

¼ cup honey

1 pinch ground cinnamon

In a small saucepan over medium-high heat, combine the apple cider and honey and bring to a simmer, stirring until the honey dissolves. Add the cinnamon and stir until dissolved. Remove from the heat and let cool. Pour the syrup into a clean storage container. Use at once, or cover and refrigerate for up to 2 weeks.

Apple Shrub

MAKES ABOUT 1½ CUPS

1 cup unfiltered apple juice or apple cider

1 apple, cored and grated (about 1 cup)

½ cup sugar

¼ cup water

¼ cup apple cider vinegar

In a saucepan, combine the apple juice, grated apple, sugar, and water. Heat over medium heat, stirring occasionally, until the sugar dissolves and the apple begins to break down, about 5 minutes. Remove from the heat and allow the mixture to cool to room temperature. Once cooled, mash the apple to release the juices.

Strain the mixture through a fine-mesh sieve or cheesecloth into a clean jar or bottle, pressing the solids to extract as much juice as possible.

Add the apple cider vinegar and stir to combine. Seal the jar and refrigerate for 3 days before using, allowing the flavors to meld. Shake the jar occasionally. Use within 2 weeks.

Pineapple-Pomegranate Shrub

MAKES ABOUT 2 CUPS

1 cup chopped fresh pineapple chunks

½ cup unsweetened pomegranate juice

½ cup sugar

⅓ cup water

¼ cup apple cider vinegar

In a saucepan, combine the chopped pineapple, pomegranate juice, sugar, and water. Heat over medium heat, stirring occasionally, until the sugar dissolves and the pineapple begins to break down, about 5 minutes. Remove from the heat and allow to cool to room temperature. Once the mixture has cooled, mash the pineapple chunks to release their juices.

Strain the mixture through a fine-mesh sieve or cheesecloth into a clean jar or bottle, pressing the solids to extract as much juice as possible.

Add the apple cider vinegar and stir to combine. Seal the jar and refrigerate for 3 days before using, allowing the flavors to meld. Shake the jar occasionally. Use within 2 weeks.

ABOUT THE AUTHOR

Kim Laidlaw is a *New York Times* best-selling cookbook author, recipe developer, and editor. She is the author or coauthor of twelve cookbooks, including bestsellers *Elvira's Cookbook from Hell*, *Yellowstone: The Official Dutton Ranch Family Cookbook*, *Tim Burton's The Nightmare Before Christmas* cookbook, and *Emily in Paris: The Official Cookbook*. She has also authored numerous Williams Sonoma cookbooks along with *Clueless: The Official Cookbook* and *The Rocky Horror Cookbook*. Kim is a seasoned recipe developer and tester working with international brands, celebrities, chefs, influencers, and authors. Her clients include Paramount, Netflix, Disney, Samuel Adams, Weber, American Girl, and more. She has managed hundreds of cookbook projects, including 2025 James Beard Award–winner *CONVIVER* and Kendall-Jackson's *SEASON*, winner of the 2019 IACP Book of the Year Award. She is a former professional baker and baking instructor at the San Francisco Cooking School and attended the California Culinary Academy.

weldon**owen**
an imprint of Insight Editions
P.O. Box 3088
San Rafael, CA 94912
www.weldonowen.com

CEO Raoul Goff
VP Publisher Roger Shaw
Executive Editor Edward Ash-Milby
Assistant Editor Kayla Belser
Managing Editor Michelle Hope
Art Director & Designer Megan Sinead Bingham
Production Design Jean Hwang
VP Manufacturing Alix Nicholaeff
Senior Production Manager Joshua Smith
Strategic Production Planner Lina s Palma-Temena

Photography by Ken Carlson (Waterbury Publications)
Food Styling by Josh Hake

Weldon Owen would also like to thank Ellen Foreman and Margaret Parrish.

ISBN: 979-8-88674-341-8

Manufactured in China by Insight Editions
10 9 8 7 6 5 4 3 2 1